PILGRIMAGE
PATHWAYS *for the*
UNITED STATES

PILGRIMAGE PATHWAYS *for the*

UNITED STATES

Creating Pilgrimage Routes to Enrich Lives, Enhance Community, and Restore Ecosystems

JAMES E. MILLS

Illustrations by Tyra Olstad

North Atlantic Books
Berkeley, California

Published by
North Atlantic Books
Berkeley, California

Illustrations by Dr. Tyra Olstad
Cover photo © Piotr Krzeslak/Shutterstock.com
Cover design by John Barnett
Book design by Happenstance Type-O-Rama

Printed in the United States of America

Pilgrimage Pathways for the United States: Creating Pilgrimage Routes to Enrich Lives, Enhance Community, and Restore Ecosystems is sponsored and published by the Society for the Study of Native Arts and Sciences (dba North Atlantic Books), an educational nonprofit based in Berkeley, California, that collaborates with partners to develop cross-cultural perspectives, nurture holistic views of art, science, the humanities, and healing, and seed personal and global transformation by publishing work on the relationship of body, spirit, and nature.

North Atlantic Books' publications are available through most bookstores. For further information, visit our website at www.northatlanticbooks.com or call 800-733-3000.

Library of Congress Cataloging-in-Publication Data

Names: Mills, James E., 1956- author.
Title: Pilgrimage pathways for the United States : creating pilgrimage routes to enrich lives, enhance community, and restore ecosystems / James E. Mills ; illustrations by Tyra Olstad.
Description: Berkeley : North Atlantic Books, [2021] | Includes bibliographical references and index.
Identifiers: LCCN 2020039481 (print) | LCCN 2020039482 (ebook) | ISBN 9781623175498 (trade paperback) | ISBN 9781623175504 (ebook)
Subjects: LCSH: Environmentalism—United States. | Spirituality—United States. | Pilgrims and pilgrimages—United States. | Trails—United States. | Humanitarianism—United States. | Communities—United States.
Classification: LCC GE197 .M557 2021 (print) | LCC GE197 (ebook) | DDC 203/.50973—dc23
LC record available at https://lccn.loc.gov/2020039481
LC ebook record available at https://lccn.loc.gov/2020039482

1 2 3 4 5 6 7 8 9 KPC 25 24 23 22 21

*For my parents, and all those who have walked
life's pathways and gone on before us*

ACKNOWLEDGMENTS

Deep thanks to my colleague Dr. Tyra Olstad for the graceful illustrations. She astounds me with her artistic and literary talents on a regular basis. I am fortunate to have her artwork included in this volume.

Daniel Boyd spent months helping me develop a better understanding of the ways pilgrimage routes might be configured here in upstate New York. He spent many hours in the field and developed a robust GIS program and methodology that could be used to help pilgrimage planners here and in places around the country.

Deb Bruce came to my rescue by her careful reading and editorial suggestions of the manuscript. Her keen sense of humor and kindness took some of the sting out of seeing my many mistakes and lapses. Any remaining errors are surely my own.

My thanks to Shayna Keyles and the rest of the staff at North Atlantic Books. It has been a great privilege and pleasure to work with such professional, passionate, and caring individuals.

None of this would have been possible without Susan Ryder, my beloved wife, who has always been at and on my side.

CONTENTS

PREFACE

Many trails can converge at the same destination. Thus it has been for me. In both my personal and professional lives, I have journeyed down different routes to reach the vision of creating new pilgrimage pathways as articulated in this book.

One of these paths has been my life as an environmentalist. Much of my time on Planet Earth has been spent walking and exploring landscapes across the US and around the world. I completed several degrees in natural resources and geography. I have taught environmental studies and issues of sustainability to thousands of students over the last thirty years. I conducted research on a wide range of environmental topics from soils to scenic rivers. For many years I served as the director of an environmental science program and helped create a new major in environmental sustainability that now enrolls well over a hundred students annually.

These experiences and training leave me acutely aware of the many environmental challenges we face today—including climate change, loss of biodiversity, pollution, and rampant resource consumption. Solving such problems will not be easy. We need to better embrace the science, but I also know that to solve these problems we need to go beyond. We will have to change ourselves and our culture. The environmental crises we face will not begin to get better until our behaviors, values, institutions, and ultimately, human landscapes are transformed in significant ways.

Another pathway I have followed in my life is more about spirit and meaning. I was brought up in and still respect my Lutheran heritage. But encounters with friends and colleagues from around the world who are Jewish, Buddhist, Hindu, Muslim, and Sikh helped me to understand that there are many faces and means to the divine. My PhD dissertation explored the notion of sacred place as it was perceived and conceived by pre-Columbian Indigenous People in the Upper Mississippi River Basin, and compared that to the notions of feng shui practitioners in South Korea and other parts of East Asia. I have taught a course on sacred space and spiritual landscapes for many years. I have been an active member of a Unitarian Universalist congregation for the last twenty years.

It is clear to me that interfaith understanding is absolutely critical in the US as our society becomes more diverse. It is also clear that something else is happening. More and more people today find that no organized religion or codified set of beliefs or rituals seems to speak to them anymore. Demographers and social scientists see a country in the not-too-distant future in which more than half of the residents claim no particular religious affiliation at all. This does not mean that Americans are no longer interested in affairs of the heart and spirit, however. What it does mean is that the US is increasingly a nation of seekers, hoping to find new ways to tend their souls. I share this sentiment as well.

Yet another avenue I continue to traverse is to better understand my own privilege in the highly unequal and unfair society that the United States has become. I am not wealthy, but I have never experienced the crushing poverty that millions of Americans deal with most of their lives. I have never had to suffer the cruel discrimination, prejudice, and violence suffered by so many Americans who are not white or Christian. Women and those who are not cisgender or heterosexual have had to navigate a hostile and often dangerous culture in ways that I can only imagine. My ongoing struggle and hope is to do what I can to make the US more like the beloved community Dr. Martin Luther King, Jr. imagined.

What does all this have to do with pilgrimage? Like most Americans, pilgrimage had little meaning or significance for me growing up. I was unaware of any pilgrimages anywhere in the United States and did not know of anyone who had ever been on a pilgrimage. It was rarely, if ever, a topic of conversation. If anything, pilgrimage might have been something I read about in history books or travel magazines.

Pilgrimage became more important to me first through an academic lens. As I began to teach and learn more about sacred space and religion, pilgrimage began to take a higher profile. I had opportunities to visit pilgrimage destinations in Vietnam, Japan, Malaysia, India, the Levant, Ireland, and France. I immersed myself in the academic literature and theoretical debates about pilgrimage in anthropology and other social sciences.

I began to wonder what it might be like to go on a pilgrimage myself. I read novels and first-person accounts. It became increasingly clear to me that pilgrimage has the power to transform and heal individuals. For many, it was one of the most important and meaningful experiences of their lives. I began to imagine myself undertaking a major pilgrimage and having similar experiences. However, I quickly realized this would be difficult if not impossible. I would probably have to go abroad to accomplish such a task, and the cultural and religious context would be quite foreign to me. Opportunities in the United States were rare or simply not compatible with my spiritual leanings.

There came a point when I realized that making new pilgrimage pathways in this country might be a way that all these life paths of mine could intersect. The US has not had a strong pilgrimage tradition in the past, but that does not mean it has to stay that way in the future. Because pilgrimage is a nearly universal practice it made sense to me that done well, pilgrimage could blossom and thrive in the United States as it has in virtually every other part of the world.

I realized too that new pilgrimages in the US should be different in significant ways. I would not want to see a growth in pilgrimage practices that caused or exacerbated environmental problems. I would not want new pilgrimages to further discriminate against marginalized communities or to privilege one religious tradition over another or exclude those with no formal affiliation. Pilgrimage that speaks to all the people of the United States on a spiritual level, while doing much to protect and restore ecosystems and enhance community, seems like a lot to ask, but after reading this book I hope you agree that it is entirely possible.

I know that others have biographies that parallel mine. Many of you continue to walk your own versions of environmental, spiritual, and social justice pathways. Perhaps the ideas that follow here will resonate with your own experience and give you hope and the means to help create a more sustainable, just, and numinous world.

Introduction

SCENARIO

It is thirty years into the future. The population of the United States has grown to around 400 million and is more religiously diverse than at any other point in history. While many Americans continue to identify as Christians there are sizable portions of the US population that practice Hinduism, Islam, Buddhism, and other world religions. Nearly half of Americans do not see themselves as being followers of any religion at all.

Landscapes across the continent continue to be transformed. Natural areas have been further diminished or lost as they have been converted into office parks, housing developments, strip malls, warehouses, agricultural fields, and other human alterations. Most cities have increased in population. While some urban areas have become vibrant and desirable places to live, many others still suffer from lack of investment, sprawl, traffic congestion, and segregation by race and class.

Rising ocean levels have resulted in significant losses of land along coastlines, and climate change has triggered ecological changes across North

America—and indeed the world. Additional plant and animal species are now extinct or are increasingly endangered. Pollution and toxic materials still threaten the health and well-being of large portions of ecosystems and human populations.

A more positive development can be discerned in many localities across the country as well. From afar or seen on satellite images, distinct corridors have emerged. These linear features emanate from hundreds of population centers across the country and many interconnect to create vast webs. Larger green spaces are often linked by these corridors, like emeralds on a necklace. On closer inspection we see that these corridors contain pathways with significant numbers of people walking along them.

What has become manifest is a continent-spanning network of communal pilgrimage pathways. From a country that had virtually no dedicated pilgrimage routes, the US now has hundreds. From a society where few citizens ever went on pilgrimage—or if they did, they went abroad—the practice has now become commonplace and local. Participation rates have soared, and many Americans of all religious backgrounds or even those with no stated affiliation now consider a pilgrimage walk to be an essential and regular part of their lives and spiritual experience.

These corridors are more than simple thoroughfares. They have created better conditions for plants and animals by stitching together and expanding fragmented habitats. Many of the pathways are designed to remediate runoff, reduce soil erosion, and protect wetland areas. These pathways lead pilgrims to numinous and liminal places that evoke spiritual awareness. There are gardens, artworks, and gathering places along the way. These pathways serve as learning laboratories, helping the pilgrims develop a rich sense of place by delving deeply into the history and ecology of their region while they are on their spiritual journeys.

THE PRESENT

The United States is in many ways at a watershed moment in its history. Studies and polls now point to an increasingly diverse group of religions being practiced along with an increasingly large portion of the population who identify with no organized religion at all, but nevertheless consider spiritual matters to be an important aspect of their lives. The implications of such a dramatic change in the religious sphere have yet to be fully comprehended. We know that it has already provoked reactionary responses, and that a few individuals would go so far as to ban certain adherents from entering the country or restrict the practice of non-Christian religions. Tolerance and even a celebration of interfaith understanding will hopefully prevail in the long term. For the time being, however, traditional denominations continue to lose members, especially as the young look for alternative experiences and new ways to tend their souls.

Religious diversification and transformation are not the only social issues we face. Many Americans still suffer from living in a society where social interaction and community building atrophy. There are historically high rates of depression, mental illness, and opioid abuse. Economic restructuring has left many without meaningful work or hope in the future. Our political institutions are under a great deal of stress, and political polarization seems to be at an unprecedented level. Racism, sexism, classism, and xenophobia continue to plague society. African American, Indigenous American, Asian

American, and Latinx communities experience discrimination and violence on a regular basis. Many Americans are unwilling or unsure how to move to a more just society.

The US is already is facing dramatic environmental crises. Foremost is climate change. The impacts of climate change for the United States and the rest of the world are increasingly apparent every day. Extreme temperatures, the increased incidence of wildfires, severe weather events, droughts and flooding, the spread of disease, and the likelihood of coastal inundation and millions of environmental refugees are just some of the daunting challenges. We are facing the loss of perhaps half of all known species on earth in what many are now referring to as the sixth great extinction. Nonrenewable natural resources are being consumed rapidly, and increased numbers of people with growing demands are not only hastening the depletion of many such resources, but severely compromising renewable resources as well.

Enter the notion of pilgrimage. While most Americans have some sense of what pilgrimage is, very few have undertaken such a journey. Pilgrimage has been thought of as something that people in other countries do, or perhaps what a few Americans might choose to do if they have the opportunity to go to another country, such as a pilgrimage to Rome or Mecca. Many US residents still think that pilgrimage is just an arcane ritual or religious activity and something not especially relevant to their own lives.

On the other hand, awareness is growing. More and more people express an interest in participating in a pilgrimage. An immediate dilemma for those interested is that there are few opportunities readily available. The US does not have a history or strong pilgrimage tradition to look to for guidance. People increasingly are intrigued by the prospect of setting out on a spiritual journey, but do not really know how to do it or exactly where to go. Catholics and Mormons do have a series of shrines or pilgrimage destinations around the country, and many opt to take advantage of such places. Other individuals understandably turn to the exotic and distant and plan trips to places such as Bali or Northern Spain. Some look for guidance from New Age practitioners and journey to places such as Sedona, Arizona. Still others travel to commemorate popular culture icons or pay tribute to those lost to war by going to places such as the Vietnam Veterans Memorial. Not many Americans immediately think of going on pilgrimage close to where they live or focusing on the journey rather than the destination.

Americans might be surprised to learn that increased pilgrimage participation and the creation of new pilgrimage pathways could be not only an individual or religious quest, but also a way to heal an increasingly fractious society and an increasingly ailing earth. One of the hallmarks of pilgrimage throughout history has been healing. Traditionally pilgrims would go on pilgrimage in hopes that they themselves or perhaps a loved one could be cured of some physical ailment, spiritual angst, or mental illness. It is possible that a pilgrimage tradition, conceived for a new era and a newly emerging culture, could continue to heal not only individuals but also begin to heal entire communities and the earth itself.

Pilgrimage is a nearly universal practice. People from all religions, all historical periods, on all continents have participated in and continue to go on pilgrimage. It is a complex and dynamic phenomenon. Around the world many pilgrimages from the past have disappeared, while many new ones have taken their place. Pilgrimages that endure have often evolved and changed, even in locales where they have taken place for centuries.

Americans have been a major exception to this pattern for the past few centuries. The US is changing rapidly, however. Americans are perhaps more ready than ever to create new pilgrimages and pilgrimage practices more in line with their emerging spiritualities and evolving cultural sensibilities.

THIS BOOK

This work is an extended argument for the creation of a network of walking pilgrimage routes across the United States. We live in a time of accelerating crises, and it is sometimes difficult to know how to navigate ourselves into a more just, humane, and sustainable future. What follows is a vision of one way we can move forward in the face of what sometimes seems like insurmountable odds.

The ideas here should be of interest especially to people who might themselves want to undertake a pilgrimage. In a broad sense, that could include most people in the US, at least at some point in their lives. Pilgrimage is something that people through the ages and around the planet have found to be deeply fulfilling and one of their most important life experiences. Americans who have gone on pilgrimages can attest to this truth. Unfortunately, most have been hampered from this activity by denominational prohibitions and lack of readily accessible, recognized sacred places. Such barriers are disappearing, however. The demand is surely growing. Americans should be more active in promoting their ability and perhaps their right to undertake a walking pilgrimage.

Environmental activists, environmental planners, and environmental officials should also find much of interest in the proposals outlined in this book. New pathways as envisioned here have the potential to reduce greenhouse gas emissions and to slow or halt the great loss of biodiversity we face. Locating walking pilgrimages near to where people live can reduce car and air transportation impacts and the pathways themselves can be designed to enhance and expand wildlife habitat, reduce soil erosion, and prevent water pollution.

Religious officials and clergy, along with leaders in the interfaith movement, may find the ideas here compelling. Many Americans, especially the young, seem less interested in traditional religious services and doctrines and are looking for new ways to encounter the divine. Pilgrimages allow for intense and embodied spiritual experiences. Group pilgrimages hold out the possibility of enhancing community and congregational bonds and strengthening commitment. Interfaith walks can do much to encourage better understanding of those who portray and worship the divine in different ways.

Pilgrimages as described here might also pique the interest of community developers and activists. There are activities and developments in this proposal that have the potential to strengthen community bonds, enhance local economic conditions, and improve people's health and well-being. Creating new pilgrimage paths and engaging in regular pilgrimage walks is a deeply communitarian exercise. Local officials may find creative new ways to invigorate and renew their beloved villages, towns, and cities.

Pilgrimage has growing appeal and offers abundant opportunities to help heal ourselves and our planet. Creating a new network of pilgrimage pathways would allow Americans to take advantage of those opportunities. I invite you now to walk with me through the following pages. Hopefully, the ideas explored here will spark your imagination and your passion for helping to create a pilgrimage pathway near where you live.

Bodh Gaya, India

2

Pilgrimage

A review of the history and extent of pilgrimage is a good place for us to begin. Pilgrimage has a rich history and many variations that can help inform the creation of new pathways and pilgrimage opportunities in the US.

We know that for thousands of years, humans around the world have left their homes and journeyed to find healing, enlightenment, forgiveness, atonement, adventure, and to seek contact with the divine. Some suffered greatly in the process, either by choice or by circumstance. They may have gone on a day trek or perhaps instead covered thousands of miles over the course of many weeks or months. Many traveled in a direct path while others circled a sacred site or shrine. Most returned home quietly while some returned to great fanfare. Whatever the details, for hundreds of millions of individuals the experience was transformational and positively affected them the rest of their lives.

The pilgrimage phenomenon is diverse and dynamic. It defies easy description and definition. It transcends individual cultures, religions, and historical periods. The common notion is that pilgrimage is a journey undertaken to a sacred or holy destination for various religious or spiritual purposes. For most people this is simply what the term means, and they do not delve any deeper into the practice or concept. However, pilgrimage can be more nuanced and complex than such a standard definition implies.

Definitions of pilgrimage abound. Some writers have put forth broad definitions that encompass a wide range of phenomena. One such attempt defines pilgrimage as "a journey to a special place, in which both the journey and the destination have spiritual significance."[1] Some writers choose to define pilgrimage broadly, but in more personal and less overtly religious terms such as "a journey undertaken by a person in quest of a place or a state that they believe to embody a valued ideal."[2] Justine Digance chooses to define pilgrimage simply as "journeys redolent with meaning."[3] Robert Macfarlane might consider pilgrimage "a more than functional act."[4] Others prefer to narrow the term to a greater degree of specificity, for example:

> *I find it helpful to define pilgrimage as a ritual journey from the quotidian realm of profane society to a sacred center, a passion-laden, hypermeaningful voyage both outwardly and inwardly, which is often steeped in symbols and symbolic actions.*[5]

The fact of the matter is, no single definition of pilgrimage meets the needs of all who talk or write about it. This is just as well. The phenomenon does not fit well into a single box.

If the concept of pilgrimage was not complicated enough already, the term is nowadays often used in metaphorical ways or in a manner that stretches conventional meanings. Is a road trip to the Baseball Hall of Fame for a sports enthusiast really a pilgrimage? Is a journey to your hometown to visit family for a holiday an annual pilgrimage? Is having survived cancer or overcome an addiction a pilgrimage? Using pilgrimage to describe any kind of journey, a trip to a special destination, or even some kind of psychological process is now commonplace.

The English word *pilgrim* has its origin in the Latin word *peregrinus*, which refers to one who is a foreigner or from abroad. The verb *peregrinate* means to travel or wander from place to place. St. Albertus Magnus, writing in the thirteenth century, thought a particular raptor was just such an avian wanderer and named it the peregrine falcon. *Pilgrimage* is a word that evolved largely within the Indo-European languages and Christian tradition of Europe. As such, we have equivalent terms such as the French *e-pèlerinage*, the Spanish *peregrinación*, the German *Pilgerfahrt*, or the Russian *palomnichestvo*. In earlier times the term was used more narrowly to describe Christians who saw themselves as temporary residents of earth traversing this material realm until they could ultimately go home to heaven. Christian motifs or hymn lyrics such as "I'm just a poor wayfaring stranger" or "I'm crossing over the River Jordan" still attest to this meaning of being a pilgrim. John Bunyan's classic 1678 work of literature entitled *Pilgrim's Progress* was written more with this sense of the word in mind. However, at least by medieval times pilgrimage had also become closely associated with a type of travel that had an actual terrestrial destination involved, such as a trip to Jerusalem or Rome.

Most other languages have a word or words that can be translated as "pilgrimage." In Hindi, for example, there is the term *tirthayatra*. *Tirtha* refers literally to a ford in a stream, but in a metaphorical sense as a place to cross over from the material to transcendent realms or simply as a sacred place where contact with the divine is possible. *Yatra* refers to a journey. The Chinese term *chao jin* means to go on a pilgrimage, while *chao shan* refers more specifically to a journey to a holy mountain. The Japanese have a number of terms including *junrei*, which is a generic term and *Henro*, which is a name for a specific pilgrimage on the island of Shikoku. The Arabic term *ziyarah* is a term for pilgrimages undertaken voluntarily, while the *Hajj* refers to the obligatory pilgrimage to Mecca that is one of the five pillars of Islam. The Maori term *hikoi manene* has associations with striding in a strange land. In fact, translation programs list an equivalent term for pilgrimage in virtually all known languages.

Humans appear to be the only species engaging in pilgrimage. Other creatures certainly migrate on a seasonal or permanent basis but presumably do so for different reasons and purposes. Like music, dance, the visual arts, prayer, or other types of ritual, pilgrimage seems to be a uniquely human practice. Although there are some notable exceptions, people in virtually all cultures and religious traditions and in all historical periods have engaged in a recognizable form of this practice. Popularity of the practice has waxed and waned between regions and historical eras but has always persisted. Carolyn Prorok writes, "[Pilgrimage] is a profoundly human endeavor that may diminish at times but never wholly disappears."[6]

Some in the mid-twentieth century thought that modernity would bring an end to pilgrimage, as most pilgrimages were seen by secular rationalists and even some learned theologians as being superstitious and backward. They were wrong. The number of pilgrims and pilgrimage destinations seems to be increasing, and pilgrimage is experiencing a revival in most parts of the world and in different religious and cultural contexts. For example, the pilgrimage of *Camino de Santiago* in Europe has seen a tremendous rise in popularity. By the early 1980s pilgrimage traffic had waned to a few thousand walkers each year. More recently the annual number of pilgrims has reached more than two hundred thousand. One estimate puts the number of people going on pilgrimage worldwide each year at more than 150 million. However, there is probably no way of knowing exact figures because of the lack of documentation and ambiguities of what constitutes pilgrimage in many cases.[7]

One apparent reason more people are going on pilgrimage is simply that there are many more people in the world each year. Even so, rates of participation seem to be increasing as well. Currently, well over two million pilgrims journey to Mecca in Saudi Arabia to participate in the *Hajj* pilgrimage on an annual basis. If the Saudi government gave out more permits, the number would jump much higher. In 1950, the number of pilgrims in Mecca was closer to fifty to one hundred thousand.

Another factor leading to increases in pilgrimage participation is improved transportation systems and visitor infrastructure. A trip to Mecca in the nineteenth century for many Muslims might have entailed weeks to months of hard travel over land or by ship. Now, most pilgrims can fly to nearby Jedda and arrive within a day of departure from their homes almost anywhere in the world. This is true for many other pilgrimages as well. For example, bus transportation has replaced walking to become the dominant way to complete the *Henro*, the pilgrimage on the Japanese island of Shikoku, where Buddhist pilgrims visit eighty-eight different temples on their 750-mile journey.

Ironically, increased formal religiosity does not always correlate with increased pilgrimage participation rates. In a few cases there is actually an inverse relationship. While many more people are going on pilgrimages in Europe, for example, fewer people there are regularly attending worship services, becoming members of organized religious bodies, or associating themselves in any way with any particular religion.

If Christian Britain is fading away, what will survive it? One answer seems to be pilgrimage. In the past decade, 30 pilgrimage routes have been created or rediscovered; holy places have seen a 14 per cent growth in visitor numbers since 2013.[8]

While pilgrimage activity is indeed increasing, it is not necessarily taking the same forms or embracing the same meanings of earlier eras. In the case of the *Camino de Santiago*, it used to be that the main purpose of the pilgrimage was to arrive at the Cathedral of Santiago de Compostela and participate in Catholic rituals there, where the bones of St. James are said to rest. A significant portion of those doing this pilgrimage today are not even Christian, and many others who might be are simply more focused on the walk itself. For these pilgrims, the bones and relics of St. James may not be associated with the same meaning or power as for a medieval Roman Catholic. Many skip the visit to the cathedral altogether or choose instead to walk a bit further to the Atlantic coast for an alternative set of rituals that are more Celtic and Pagan in nature.[9] This shift in meaning and practice is typical of other pilgrimages as well. Pilgrimage practice and meaning have always evolved and changed and apparently continue to do so today.

Suffice it to say that pilgrimage is alive and well in the twenty-first century. We appear to be in an era of revived and new pilgrimages and increased participation rates—whatever the reasons or new forms might be.

HISTORICAL OVERVIEW

Archaeological evidence suggests that the first pilgrimages might have taken place long ago. If the presence of a site of significant ritual activity indicates that people also might have traveled some distance to get to such places, then we can say that pilgrimages go back at least eleven thousand years. Archaeologists seem to be pushing back the dates of the earliest ritual activity, and there is debate whether it could have been forty thousand or seventy thousand years ago, or even further back in time. It is at least fair to say that modern *Homo sapiens sapiens* and perhaps earlier or other human ancestors have been participating in ritual activities for thousands of years, some of which might have included a pilgrimage component.

Before 9000 BC human groups were mostly nomadic and lived by hunting, fishing, gathering, and scavenging. There were few permanent settlements. Even so, we know that mortuary practices and beliefs in an afterlife were developing. Certain locales and landscape features acquired meaning and religious significance. Humans were developing complex symbolic systems and languages. People were already producing visual arts and music. An awareness of the unseen world or the world within was growing. Some of the key components for pilgrimage were well established.

One of the most extraordinary archaeological finds in recent decades is Göbekli Tepe, found in modern Turkey. The site consists of around two hundred vertical stones arranged in twenty concentric circles. Some of the stones reach a height of sixteen feet and weigh between seven and ten tons. Many have carved images on them. While a definitive interpretation is yet to be determined, the emerging consensus is that this site is the first known temple complex on earth. It was constructed by nomadic hunters and gatherers, beginning about eleven thousand years ago. It is postulated that these people came to construct and then visit the site on pilgrimages, from a radius of at least a hundred miles away, to perform rituals.[10] If this interpretation is true, then it is evidence that pilgrimages were being developed even before people began to settle into permanent settlements and take up farming.

Göbekli Tepe, Turkey

Once humans did settle down and take up an agricultural way of life, it did not stop them from pursuing pilgrimages. A prevailing theory of why people settled down in the first place was because they wanted to practice religion collectively. Çatalhöyük, one of the first known cities in the world, was probably built to accommodate such a religious community. Farming simply became necessary to support their religious habits. Although in the case of Çatalhöyük, this meant that those particular individuals no longer had to travel to a sacred destination, creating such a religious center likely attracted many nonresidents as well.

Another fascinating archaeological find can be found in the Orkney Islands off the north coast of the Scottish mainland. The Orkneys supported a vigorous and substantial Neolithic human population. Those individuals constructed various features we have been aware of for some time, such as standing stone circles and passage tombs. In 2002 a new ceremonial center referred to as the Ness of Brodgar was discovered. The Ness consisted of a number of stone buildings, thick surrounding walls, and substantial ceremonial structures—all constructed more than five thousand years ago. It was subsequently used for a millennium. People from around the islands as well as from the mainland came to this site for ritual activities century after century. They returned to their various homes with artifacts and probably ideas from this and other nearby sites.[11]

Other Neolithic and later ceremonial centers arose in many other places as well. By twenty-five hundred years ago, we can identify likely pilgrimage destinations across the globe. Such centers had been constructed from the coasts of Peru to the riverbanks of Mesopotamia, from the islands of the Mediterranean to the deserts of the Indus Valley and the hills of the Loess Plateau in China. Many ceremonial sites were constructed on a grand scale, with massive temples, plazas, and other features.

Hinduism, the third largest religion today in terms of the number of adherents, had its origins well over three thousand years ago. By two thousand years ago, many Hindu pilgrimages had already developed throughout the Indian subcontinent. Several passages in the *Mahābhārata* (circa 300 BC) deal with pilgrimage. The city of Banaras or Varanasi, one of the premier destinations even today, was attracting pilgrims more than two thousand years ago. India in the twenty-first century still contains a rich tapestry of Hindu pilgrimages and has one of the highest participation rates in the world.[12] The *Kumbh Mela,* arguably the largest gathering of humankind in the world, will attract tens of millions of Hindu pilgrims to the riverbanks of northern India every twelve years. *Kumbh Mela* roughly translates as "an assembly around the water of immortality."

Buddhism, Christianity, and Islam—the three largest universalizing religions today—all had their beginnings roughly between 550 BC and 650 AD. Adherents to these religions now account for well over half the people alive in the world today. The start and ensuing growth of these religions ushered in a new chapter of pilgrimage. Pilgrimage traditions developed in all three of these religions, despite the fact that only Islam mentions pilgrimage as an important component. Nevertheless, large numbers of Buddhists, Christians, and Muslims began and have continued to journey as a religious practice. Significant locations associated with the Buddha, Jesus, and the Prophet Mohammed initially generated the greatest pilgrimage flows. Pilgrimages to Bodh Gaya and related sites in northern India and Nepal for Buddhists, Jerusalem and the Holy Land for Christians, and Mecca and Medina for Muslims still compel millions of individuals to go to these religious hearths where these founding figures lived out their lives and significant events occurred.

Each of these religious traditions in turn expanded and diversified their repertoire of pilgrimage destinations over the centuries following their beginnings. There are now thousands of shrines, temples, caves, stupas, mountains, and other sites throughout south, east, and southeast Asia—and even in other parts of the world that draw Buddhist pilgrims. Besides the Holy Land and Jerusalem, Christians now journey to destinations such as Rome, Mexico City, Lourdes, Mount Athos, and an untold number of other churches, shrines, and natural features. In addition to Mecca and Medina, Shiite Muslims will flock to shrines in Isfahan, Karbala, and other places. Many Muslims will also visit Jerusalem *(Al-Quds)* and many will otherwise attend large gatherings, such as the *Bishwa Ijtema* in Bangladesh,[13] or visit shrines from West Africa to Java.

Pilgrimages are also associated with Indigenous groups and more local or regional religious traditions, although perhaps less well documented than those associated with global and universalizing religions. Many have continued to operate in various parts of the world up through the modern era. Individuals from Indigenous groups in North and South America along with those in Sub-Saharan Africa and parts of Asia were undertaking pilgrimages, perhaps for thousands of years. Zuni Salt Lake in present-day New Mexico attracted Indigenous pilgrims for centuries before and after European colonization, for example. Sites in coastal Peru drew Indigenous pilgrims at least a millennium before the Spanish conquest.[14]

In the roughly five-hundred-year period between 1500 and 2000 AD, European Christians were successful in colonizing or dominating most other parts of the world, including most of North and South America, Sub-Saharan Africa, South and Southeast Asia, and Oceania. As a result many

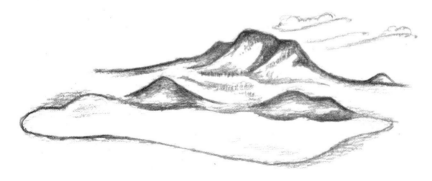

Zuni Salt Lake, New Mexico

local and Indigenous pilgrimages in these areas disappeared as Indigenous populations plummeted in the New World, and Christian conversion was widely imposed on the remaining inhabitants—from Tierra del Fuego to the Arctic Circle and from Cape Town to Manila. Millions of Africans were captured and forced into slavery in the New World.

Indigenous pilgrimage did not entirely disappear, however. Some pilgrimages developed into syncretic traditions that blended Indigenous practices with Christianity, such as in the pilgrimage to the Sanctuary of the Lord of Qoyllur Rit'i in the Andean region.[15] Devotees of the María Lionza religion, which is a blend of Catholic, West African, and other customs, go on pilgrimage to Sorte Mountain in Venezuela. Haitians go on pilgrimages to such places as the Saut-d'Eau waterfall and engage in rituals that blend voodoo and Christianity. Members of the Shembe sect in South Africa, which incorporates both Christian and Indigenous Zulu practices and beliefs, go on an annual pilgrimage to the mountain Nhlangakazi (aka Mount Campion).

Pilgrimage is clearly something close to a universal human phenomenon. It has been taking place for thousands of years, and does not seem to be going away anytime soon. People who speak different languages, practice different religions, live different lifestyles, and experience varying levels of economic development all go on pilgrimage. They journey in vastly different environments, from densely populated areas to wilderness, from mountains to seashores, and from forests to deserts. There is something deeply significant about pilgrimage and we know that for many it is one of the most important experiences of their lives. Seyyed Hossein Nasr claims that pilgrimage is universal and found in all religious contexts. When denied for whatever reason, people find alternatives or substitutes. It is human nature.[16]

MOTIVATIONS

One of the most striking aspects of pilgrimage is that, with a few exceptions, it is largely a matter of personal choice whether or not to go on a pilgrimage. Most of the world's religions do not require it, and many religious authorities have even discouraged the practice at least at some point in their histories. Even in Islam, where there is an obligatory aspect, only a small portion of Muslims will ever have the opportunity to participate in the *Hajj*. There are well over a billion Muslims in the world, and less than three million are allowed permits to participate in the annual *Hajj*. In almost all other traditions, individuals must decide for themselves that a pilgrimage is something that they want to do rather than something they ought to do. Some individuals might be coerced or cajoled into doing a pilgrimage by their religious authorities or by families and friends, but most pilgrims undertake their pilgrimage as a clear act of volition.

What is it about pilgrimage that makes individuals believe it is worth perhaps weeks or months of their life, a substantial financial commitment, and undergoing what might turn out to be a difficult and rigorous physical ordeal? There are many reasons given by pilgrims as to why they think such sacrifices are worth it. Ian Reader lists at least twenty reasons articulated by Japanese pilgrims he interviewed for going on pilgrimage.[17] One of the main reasons is that people want to memorialize the dead or to contemplate their own mortality. Some pilgrims seek atonement or forgiveness. Others take on the journey because they are at a transition point in their lives—such as being recently unemployed, retired, married, or having graduated from school or college. They feel the need to do something to help them mourn, celebrate, or face their future. Still other pilgrims say they are simply there to enjoy nature, get away from it all, and relax and get healthy. Many have overt religious reasons and believe they are gaining spiritual merit. Often, pilgrims take the occasion of pilgrimage to pray for health or worldly benefits for themselves or loved ones. Some go to get away from work and family while others instead go to connect with colleagues and family members. Most individuals bring home a scroll that documents their journey, thereby gaining status and authority. Others just want a new experience or are accompanying a friend or spouse.

Almost all pilgrims expect and often achieve some type of personal or spiritual transformation. Jean Dalby Clift and Wallace B. Clift claim that pilgrimage is a Jungian archetype and that pilgrims throughout the world and throughout history have fairly common motivations for undertaking pilgrimages.[18] These motivations include wanting to see the places where central figures of their faith tradition lived, or where religiously significant events occurred. Somehow being in the actual place where their revered religious figure had been or where a significant event occurred brings greater understanding and closeness. Many go to be in communication with the divine and to express their love of God. Pilgrims go to request pardon, give thanks, or ask for health and healing. Clift and Clift claim that many go simply out of curiosity or to have new experiences. They also note that death and themes of mortality are quite common.

Pilgrims typically do not have a single or simple motivation. Most pilgrims have at least several reasons to go on pilgrimage. Some are overt and apparent, and some may not be clear even to the pilgrims themselves. Motivations also typically include a mix of sacred and secular reasons (e.g., to worship at a shrine, ask for both forgiveness and health, and relax and sightsee along the way). Possibly, the more reasons a person has for going on a pilgrimage, the more likely it is that they will go. Of course, there is a degree of passion as well. For some, the singular possibility to encounter a divine presence might be the only reason and reason enough to undergo even the most difficult and demanding journey.

PILGRIMAGE IN POPULAR CULTURE, LITERATURE, AND FILM

Nowadays there are hundreds of books about pilgrimage written for popular audiences. Most authors explore their personal experience and search for meaning. The *Camino* pilgrimage alone has inspired dozens and dozens of such works. Some of these books are denominational in nature, but most are written by people with no stated or apparent affiliation. Many of these works are essentially travelogues while others use their pilgrimage experience to explore the meaning of life, give advice to readers, or promote their perspective or worldview. Well-known works in this vein include Phil Cousineau's book, *The Art of Pilgrimage: The Seeker's Guide to Making Travel Sacred,*[19] and Rosemary Mahoney's work, *The Singular Pilgrim: Travels on Sacred Ground.*[20]

The large number of authors and the expanding volume of such works gives further evidence that pilgrimage is a compelling topic, with a growing audience interested in learning more about it or perhaps anxious for advice on how to begin or where to go to find the best route.

Artists of one sort of the other have also used their skills and insights to bring greater appreciation and understanding of the practice. Novelists and filmmakers in particular have been intrigued by pilgrimage and some of the world's classic works revolve around this theme.

Literary works about pilgrimage are numerous and provide another way of expressing the attraction and experience of being a pilgrim. Tellingly, some of the earliest novels ever written focus on pilgrimage. One of the first novels in English is Geoffrey Chaucer's *The Canterbury Tales,* which tells the stories of individuals who have made the pilgrimage to Canterbury to be in close proximity to the remains of Thomas Becket. The Japanese work entitled *The Narrow Road to the Deep North,* also known as *The Narrow Road to the Interior,* by Matsuo Bashō, was written in the late 1600s. This is essentially a travelogue, but it contains many poetic, philosophical, and artistic elements and nowadays is considered a literary classic. In China there is a work entitled *Journey to the West,* by Wu Cheng'en. This novel was written in the sixteenth century but was based on a much earlier account, *Great Tang Records on the Western Regions,* written by Xuanzang during the Tang Dynasty, describing an actual pilgrimage across China and into India.

Many modern writers and filmmakers continue this tradition, and pilgrimage is a common theme in many works today. *The Way,* a popular film, tells the story that takes place among pilgrims on the *Camino.*[21] Rachel Joyce's novel *The Unlikely Pilgrimage of Harold Fry* is the quirky story of one man's unintended pilgrimage across the breadth of England.[22] Both of these works have developed large audiences of readers in the US and have brought wider attention to the idea of pilgrimage. Such works make pilgrimage personal and compelling.

3

Pilgrimage in the United States

Clearly, pilgrimages have been taking place for thousands of years, by people around the world who speak different languages and practice different religions. Humans have gone on pilgrimages to high mountains, centers of civilization, shrines in rural areas, and gatherings along rivers or in deserts. Some have gone long distances and others have stayed closer to home, but large numbers of people in all historical periods and of virtually all belief systems have gone on pilgrimage.

One glaring exception to this generalization might be the United States, over the course of the last three hundred years.

Wilber Zelinsky noted a number of ways that the US religious landscape was unusual, even quite exceptional by world standards.[1] He claimed that whatever might have been sacred to Indigenous Americans in the landscape before 1492 was largely obliterated or ignored by the Europeans who came in large numbers in the centuries that followed. He believed that there had not been enough time for European Americans to develop a new network of sacred places that might be found in places such as Europe or India.

I would agree that the US is indeed unusual and even quite exceptional by global and historical standards—notable by an absence rather than a presence. It's not that the United States doesn't have any pilgrimages to sacred places. We can point to a number of Catholic shrines, Indigenous destinations, and Mormon sites for example. It is just that we have virtually no dedicated pilgrimage routes and relatively few pilgrimage destinations, given our large population and extensive territory. Low pilgrimage participation rates in the US in the last three hundred years stand out in contrast to other parts of the world and other historical periods.

It is not so much a matter of time that is needed for the identification of sacred places and the development of pilgrimages. Three of the most famous and popular pilgrimage destinations in Europe all began relatively recently. The Catholic shrine at Lourdes in France developed after Bernadette Soubirous had several encounters with the Virgin Mary near that site in 1858. Pilgrimages to Fatima in Portugal began after similar meetings with Mary by a group of children in 1917. Six individuals conversed with Mary in Medjugorje, Bosnia, in 1981. Notably, many pilgrimages have developed throughout Latin America over the past several hundred years, and this region experienced a European takeover as well. Around the world, new pilgrimages are regularly emerging. This all suggests that there are other barriers and factors involved besides time that have hindered the identification of sacred places and the development of pilgrimages in the United States.

One of the main reasons the United States never developed at least an overtly religious and robust pilgrimage tradition is that ever since the European conquest, the largest number of individuals in the US population and most of the people in positions of power have identified themselves as Protestants. As recently as 1955, about 70% of the US population identified as Protestant.[2] This is no longer true, but together, mainline and evangelical Protestant denominations account for a bit more than 40% of the US population and still can be considered the single largest religious group.

Protestantism began in Europe in no small part as a reaction to the excesses of pilgrimage in the Catholic tradition of the Late Middle Ages. Protestants abhorred the greed and corruption that plagued many shrines and pilgrimages at the time, such as the selling of indulgences and the licentious behavior of some priests and pilgrims. They dismissed the significance and sanctity of saints. Many shrines and Catholic churches were lavishly decorated and statuary was common. Protestants perceived this as idolatrous and decadent. They proceeded to destroy buildings, relics, and icons in a number of places. Protestants were opposed to the notion that by going on pilgrimage, a person could earn merit or forgiveness, as that contradicted the basic principle of God's grace. Protestants were suspicious of embodied rituals and got rid of many of the Catholic sacraments. They opted for a more austere worship experience. Priests were seen as unnecessary intermediaries between the individual and God. They were disposed of, diminished, or demoted. The Protestant Reformation under King Henry VIII in England, for example, led directly to the destruction of monasteries, the persecution and execution of Catholic clerics and laity alike, and the cessation of pilgrimages that had been taking place to destinations such as Walsingham and Canterbury. Martin Luther, the first and foremost of the Protestant leaders, was not one to mince words and famously wrote:

All pilgrimages should be stopped. There is no good in them: no commandment enjoins them, no obedience attaches to them. Rather do these pilgrimages give countless occasions to commit sin and to despise God's commandments.[3]

The leaders of Protestant movements that emerged in the seventeenth and eighteenth centuries in Europe embraced Luther's general stance on pilgrimage. Many of these individuals and their followers left Europe and either continued in their traditions or developed new forms of Protestantism once they arrived in North America. Given this heritage, it is not surprising that most US Protestants have been unlikely to recognize, to create, or to have participated in any kind of terrestrial pilgrimage over the past three hundred years.

The founding fathers of the United States and many of its citizens, besides being Protestant, were also greatly affected by the ideas and ideals of the Enlightenment. Rationality and empiricism were increasingly elevated over emotion and belief. Miraculous events and most anything supernatural were increasingly viewed with skepticism. Religions were certainly acknowledged and accepted, but a clear separation of church and state was built into the US constitution. Pilgrimages in the US have never had any kind of state support or recognition that has been enjoyed by pilgrimages in other places and historical periods.

A further reason why Americans did not develop a strong pilgrimage tradition, even if they had wanted to, is that for the most part there are not many religious hearth areas near at hand. The places where the founding figures of world religions lived and significant formative events occurred tend to have a special attraction for pilgrims even to this day. Christianity, as well as Islam, Judaism, Buddhism, Hinduism, Sikhism, and other major world religions all originated in Asia. Until recently, Americans could not easily visit Jerusalem or other possible destinations such as Mecca, Bodh Gaya, Banaras, Mount Kailash, or Amritsar. The challenges of distance, linguistic differences, and expense were—or in many cases still are—too great for the majority of US residents.

There are certainly exceptions in the United States. There are over 126 shrines that annually attract several million Catholic visitors.[4] The Basilica of the National Shrine of Mary, Help of Christians at Holy Hill in Wisconsin, for example, attracts over five hundred thousand people each year. El Santuario de Chimayó, a small chapel in northern New Mexico, is the destination of tens of thousands of pilgrims each year during Holy Week; and many more pilgrims, tourists, and the curious at other times of the year. The Basilica of the National Shrine of the Immaculate Conception in Washington, DC, hosts over a million visitors—if not pilgrims—annually.

There are non-Catholic examples as well. The Church of Jesus Christ of Latter-day Saints (LDS) began in the US and Mormons go on pilgrimage to important sites associated with Joseph Smith, Brigham Young, and the migration of the faithful from New York to Utah. Some Indigenous American groups have created new pilgrimages or have pilgrimage destinations that have either survived the conquest and occupation or have been revived in the last few decades. Many Lakota, for example, will still sojourn in the Black Hills; and Diné will still visit the four sacred mountains that define their homeland and cosmos. Some immigrant Hindu, Buddhist, and other religious groups are in the process of creating or re-creating pilgrimages that echo those from their homelands.[5]

In the United States the emphasis is typically on the destination and the focus is most often a building or construction of some sort. Pilgrimage destinations today generally have no specified or predetermined routes associated with them. Most people arrive by automobile from various directions and locations. Whatever road or freeway you take to get to a Mormon or Catholic shrine in the US is not a major consideration and finding a place to park your vehicle might be your only real transportation concern.

From another point of view altogether, we might say that Americans are not all that exceptional after all. Americans might in fact go on pilgrimage as much as any other group of people. A number of authors contend that sacred space for many people in the United States is actually less focused on shrines and buildings and is instead more centered on nature, and especially wilderness. Wilderness as sacred space has been expressed in the writings of a number of the transcendentalists and individuals such as Henry David Thoreau and John Muir. Many modern writers agree.[6] The idea of wilderness and the notion of the sublime are closely associated in Western civilization since at least the eighteenth century. Therefore, to the extent that Americans truly believe that wilderness is a kind of sacred space and then visit these wilderness areas, it could be argued that they de facto go on a pilgrimage each time they leave civilization behind to relocate themselves in what they perceive to be the untouched and sacred mountains, deserts, forests, and other wild areas of this country.

From yet another angle we might conceive of American religion or sense of the sacred as being more broadly civic. Juan Eduardo Campo writes that sacred sites so conceived are typified by their "interconnection of God and country, commemoration of heroes (legendary and otherwise) and martyrs, and the attribution of patriotic significance to the natural landscape."[7] If these qualities do indeed create a kind of sacred space, then visits to destinations such as Mount Rushmore, the Washington Mall, Revolutionary and Civil War battlefields, and sites such as Pearl Harbor and other war memorials might also be considered ways that Americans have gone and continue to go on pilgrimage. Since the terrorist attacks, many consider the 9/11 Memorial and Museum in New York City as a sacred destination. The annual number of visitors at these attractions runs into the millions.

Some US citizens might see America as a whole as sacred, and the idea is not so much to *get* somewhere, but simply to *be* on the road. Americans might be more attracted to sacred *space* rather than sacred *place*. The frontier mentality was strong for many years and at least since the automobile era, there has been a deep-seated desire to be mobile and free. The open road as exemplified by Route 66 has generated its own set of stories. Charles Kuralt developed a whole series of TV segments broadcast on the *CBS Evening News* for many years that documented his journeys from place to place, allowing millions of Americans at least vicariously to be "On the Road." William Least Heat-Moon wrote a best-selling book about his adventures on the backroads of America that he referred to as "Blue Highways" in his book by the same name, because on typical highway maps those indicated in blue were smaller and less traveled. John Steinbeck's book *Travels with Charley: In Search of America* was both a travelogue and a meditation on his own mortality. It made it to #1 on the *New York Times* best-seller list in nonfiction. Many Americans simply aspire to drive or bike all the way across the country or to visit every single state.

"Dharma Bums" was the term used by Jack Kerouac (in his book by the same name) and other famous Beat writers and poets to refer to themselves. They strove for purposeful placelessness by driving aimlessly around the United States in order to achieve a kind of Buddhist mindfulness. Although such a Beat activity did not catch on in the popular imagination, each year millions of ordinary Americans do indeed take off down the road in their

recreational vehicles and campers. There are no doubt destinations involved, but much of the appeal of this type of travel is simple mobility. Perhaps free movement alone with no obvious destination fulfills some of the functions of more traditional pilgrimage for many Americans.

Yet another phenomenon that might be considered a type of American pilgrimage today are walk-a-thons that raise funds for charitable causes. Such events are common and occur in most US cities, college campuses, and high schools. There are now walks to support finding a cure for various types of cancer, to fight other diseases, to end hunger, or to support any number of other such causes. Rebecca Solnit writes:

> *These fund-raising walks have become the mainstream American version of pilgrimage. In many ways they have traveled far from its original nature, notable in the evolution from devoutly appealing to divine intervention to pragmatically asking friends and family for money. And yet, however banal these walks are, they retain much of the content of the pilgrimage: the subject of health and healing, the community of pilgrims, and the earning through suffering or at least exertion.*[8]

Finally, it should also be noted that many Americans actually do go on more traditional and overtly religious pilgrimages. It is just that they go outside the country to do so. Many walkers today on routes such as the *Camino de Santiago* and pilgrims at shrines in Europe such as Lourdes, Fatima, and St. Peter's Basilica in Rome are in fact US citizens. Other Americans will visit Jewish, Christian, and Muslim sites in the Levant. A select number of Muslim Americans will go on the *Hajj* each year. Increasingly, US citizens can also be found on pilgrimages in Japan, India, and elsewhere. There are hundreds of travel agencies that cater to US citizens who might be interested in going abroad on a pilgrimage, as evidenced by their literature and advertising. There is little data on how many Americans this involves, but the number is not trivial. We know that the number of US citizens on the *Camino* in the last few years has annually exceeded ten thousand.

Bruce Feiler produced a documentary film series on pilgrimage entitled *Sacred Journeys.*[9] It features various Americans who decide to go on pilgrimage. These films have been aired on public television stations across the country and have been viewed by millions. Significantly, all of the films are about Americans going on pilgrimages outside of the United States. Pilgrimages explored in the films are the *Kumbh Mela* in India, *Osun-Osogbo* in Nigeria, the *Hajj* in Saudi Arabia, Jerusalem in the Levant, the *Henro* in Japan, and Lourdes in France. Perhaps for Feiler there were just not enough US pilgrimage destinations to choose from, or they were for whatever reason just not as compelling as those taking place in other countries.

DEMOGRAPHIC AND CULTURAL CHANGES IN THE UNITED STATES

Changes are taking place in the United States that have the potential to dramatically alter the way Americans create or recognize sacred places, and the degree to which they might participate in associated pilgrimages in the future. Quite possibly, the days of US exceptionalism in terms of pilgrimage might be coming to an end.

One of the most dramatic changes is in the area of religious affiliation. There are two relevant aspects to this change. The first is that although Protestants still make up a large part of the US population, the country today is much more diverse in this regard than it has ever been. Studies by the Pew Research Center highlight these changes. The portion of the US populace identifying as Protestant continues to decline. Reported affiliation with mainline Protestant groups went from 18.1% in 2007 to 14.7% in 2014, and evangelical denominations went from 26.3% in 2007 to 25.4% in 2014.[10] A 2019 poll showed that adult Americans identifying as Christian of any denomination was about 65%, down significantly from about 90% in the late 1970s.[11] Increasing proportions of the population identify as Buddhists, Hindus, Muslims, and members of dozens of other religions. The portion of the US population affiliated with non-Christian religions went from near zero in 1948 to 4.7% in 2007, then to 5.9% in 2014, and approaching 7% in 2019.

Americans often don't stay with one denomination, in any case. A large number of individuals in the US population have switched their affiliation once or more at some point in their adult life. People now are also much more willing and able to marry people from different denominations or even entirely different religions. Denominational or religious affiliation seems to be less central to an individual's identity, and marrying someone from another religion or denomination is not as strong of a taboo as it once might have been. Furthermore, for many people their religious identity is not well described by a single unwavering category. Many individuals today see themselves as not this or that, but as something in between and more fluid.

The second aspect of this changing religious landscape is that the fastest growing group in the US population is made up of those people who identify with no organized religion or religious denomination at all. Pew surveys show a dramatic increase in this group from about 3% in the 1970s, to 16.1% in 2007, to 22.8% in 2014, and closer to 26% in 2019. This means that the no religion—or "nones" or "dones" (individuals who once claimed an affiliation but no longer do)—today make up a larger group than either Catholics or mainline or evangelical Protestants. This is unprecedented in American history, and the trend shows no sign of abating or slowing down in the near future. There are many reasons why this change is taking place, but it is significant that these trends are at least in part age related. Young adults and youth today act very differently when it comes to religion, compared to their parents and grandparents. In the 2019 survey only 49% of Millennials (born between 1981 and 1996) identify as Christian versus 76% of the Baby Boomers (born between 1946 and 1964).

Some of the individuals who choose "none of the above" consider themselves to be atheists or agnostics. This subgroup, however, is relatively small. The majority of "nones" instead see religion and spirituality more as an individually determined aspect of who they are. The phrase "spiritual but not religious" is often used. Many such individuals want to be able to mix and match beliefs or develop their own. Some chafe at being compelled to accept a particular doctrine or to make financial contributions to a religious organization. Many people do not want to make formal or long-term commitments to any group. Others are frustrated by what they see as the failures and hypocrisy of organized religion. Nevertheless, they maintain that spiritual matters remain important in their lives.

Another demographic change, apart from religious affiliation, that will possibly affect pilgrimage participation rates in the future is that the overall age structure of the US population is changing. The average age is going up and greater portions of the population are in the older cohorts. What is happening in many pilgrimages around the world is that people in their fifties and sixties are one of the most likely age groups to participate. Reasons why this might be are that such individuals are often experiencing many transitions in their lives and are facing a number of concerns about aging—perhaps their ultimate passing. Many are nearing or at the point of retirement. Even so, people in developed countries, at least, often remain relatively healthy into their seventies and eighties. They are more financially able to travel and often have fewer family obligations that would prevent them from undergoing such journeys.

CHANGING PERCEPTIONS OF
SACRED PLACES AND PILGRIMAGE

Changes in attitude, affiliation, and demography are already affecting the creation or recognition of sacred places in the United States. New religious ideas and alternative spiritualities and sentiment are finding expression in many rituals and behaviors that at least approximate pilgrimage. The Protestant population is declining, and even increasingly embracing pilgrimage. There appears to be a growing interest in identifying or creating new kinds of sacred space and spiritual landscapes. Many individuals are now looking for more embodied, intense, and experiential rituals and events. Americans are increasingly intrigued by pilgrimage as a spiritual practice even if they are not entirely sure how to go about it. Evidence of this can be seen on several fronts.

Some Americans simply decide to go it on their own. They might choose to go abroad—to sites across Europe or increasingly to pilgrimages in Japan, Africa, and elsewhere. Others create self-defined pilgrimages to destinations that have personal significance. Destinations vary from person to person.

Some of these pilgrims may visit ancestral homes or homelands. Many people take pilgrimages in which they are the sole traveler. The route, destination, and timing are all individually determined. Some places may attract such loners more than others. However, for many Americans going alone is either their preferred way to go on pilgrimage, or because the US does not generally support more collective pilgrimages this is the only option available to them.

Other individuals today in the United States either refer to themselves or are labeled by others as New Age religionists. A subset of the "nones" or "spiritual but not religious" might fall into this category. Even people who are affiliated with traditional religions and denominations might occasionally participate in New Age activities and practices. What it means to be a New Age enthusiast is not always clear. Generally, it means that practitioners don't celebrate or pray to the Abrahamic God, although some believe that other divine beings such as angels or devas inhabit the universe. Some such entities might be channeled, and therefore communication with divine or spiritual beings is possible. There is much discussion of the evolution of human consciousness and dramatic societal changes. New Age enthusiasts most often speak of a somewhat undefined universal power or force that energizes people and places. Practitioners often seek or offer alternative health practices such as acupuncture or Reiki. Some New Age enthusiasts promote the recognition of Gaia—or the earth itself as a kind of superorganism.

New Age rituals and practices can include elements from Buddhism, Taoism, Hinduism, Indigenous American religions, Paganism, Wicca, and any number of other traditions. Practitioners might try dowsing or hire a feng shui practitioner to help them arrange their living spaces or gardens. Some attest to the presence of ley lines and perhaps the existence of visitors from other planets and star systems. There is an implicit sense that some places are indeed sacred or have a special force or energy associated with them, and that these places are not just socially constructed. Little formal organization and no particular doctrine or creed are universally agreed upon. There are no obvious churches, shrines, or temples; although there are a number of therapists, consultants, guides, retreat centers, and commercial establishments

33

that target this population. Rainbow Gatherings, which often involve many New Age practices, occur on an annual basis and can attract over 30,000 participants to various national forests around the United States.

At least two specific US places have become specifically associated with New Age practices and are considered sacred space by many such individuals. One of these locations is Sedona, Arizona. The landscape around Sedona has long been noted for its dramatic red rock formations and desert scenery. Over sixty feature-length Western movies have been filmed in this area. In the last several decades, Sedona has also attracted people who think that some of these rock formations funnel or concentrate a kind of cosmic or divine energy. These features and locations that do so are referred to as vortexes, as initially named and identified by psychics Dick Sutphen and Page Bryant in the late 1970s.[12]

Over three million tourists now visit Sedona in a typical year. How many of these visitors might be classified as New Age pilgrims rather than tourists is difficult to discern. Various estimates run from 10–60% of this total.[13] If so, then more than a hundred thousand and perhaps more than a million New Age pilgrims each year go on tours to these vortexes or stay at the multitude of healing and spiritual retreat centers in the area. They hope, just like more traditional pilgrims around the world, to encounter an energetic force and benefit or be transformed in some way.

For New Age pilgrim-tourists and practitioners, Sedona is a power spot, a material manifestation of energetic consciousness. For them, it is a material manifestation of hope, harmony, and universal goodness and abundance. It is an expression of collective human consciousness and a place that facilitates a turn inward to the divine Self.[14]

Similarly, Mount Shasta in northern California has experienced a growth in interest and speculation from New Age practitioners due to its perceived spiritual qualities. Thousands of New Age seekers go to Mount Shasta in search of healing, to meditate, to practice yoga, to engage in various rituals, and to encounter spiritual masters of one persuasion or another. A scene on the slopes of Mount Shasta was described as follows:

> *Crystals were placed in and near the water, particularly Panther Spring, sacred to the Wintu Tribe. Prayer flags were tied to the tree branches, and pictures and poems were left on small rock altars in the meadows and near springs. The crisscrossing trails led to altars. ... Nude sunbathing, drumming, and chanting were frequent activities nearby.*[15]

Clearly, many New Age enthusiasts are intrigued with specific places and will often travel long distances to locales that they believe offer contact with the divine as they understand and perceive it to be. They go to be with other like-minded seekers. The activities they engage in or rituals they perform once they arrive at these places are eclectic and evolving.

A different set of newly defined sacred places that have generated what could be called pilgrimages are sites associated with popular culture celebrities. The one place that has received the most attention in this regard is Graceland, the home and now final resting place of Elvis Presley in Memphis, Tennessee. Over a half a million visitors tour the house and grounds each year. On the anniversaries of Elvis's death, great processions form.

Mount Shasta, California

Many of the behaviors taking place at Graceland mirror those at more traditional pilgrimage destinations—including prayer, singing, lighting candles, putting flowers on his grave, buying souvenirs, and engaging in various group activities. A portion of Central Park near to where Beatles musician John Lennon was murdered is now known as Strawberry Fields, named after the song Lennon wrote of the same name. This place similarly attracts large numbers of Lennon fans and admirers each year. Various commemorations and rituals are held at the site. Fans come to imagine a new world, especially on the anniversary of Lennon's death.[16] Yet another example is the Oregon location where athlete Steve Prefontaine died in an automobile accident. This site has become the destination of thousands each year. This place is now referred to as Pre's Rock and attracts athletes and fans of this man who did much to popularize long-distance running as a sport.

The Vietnam Veterans Memorial in Washington, DC, has become what many would consider a significant pilgrimage destination. Maya Lin's design of the monument is unusual in that that are few overt symbols or patriotic messages. God is not evoked. There are no statues of heroes hoisting the flag or bravely charging the foe. Instead, it is a simple V-shaped wall sunk down into the ground with a walkway running along it. The wall lists the names of all those Americans who lost their lives in that conflict inscribed in black granite. In spite of, or perhaps because of its minimalist design, the memorial attracts hundreds of thousands each year. Visitors bring their own interpretations, memories, and meanings to the place.

An annual trip to the Vietnam Veterans Memorial organized by the Run for the Wall group is particularly notable. Hundreds of motorcycle riders every year make a ten-day pilgrimage to Washington, DC, and "the Wall" all the way from California. This annual event has been taking place since 1989.[17] The group for many years largely consisted of Vietnam veterans who rode to commemorate fallen comrades and those missing in action. The purpose has also been to help the veterans themselves better cope with their own injuries and scars—both physical and mental—from that conflict. Their philosophy as posted on their website reads: "We strive to maintain a safe, supportive and private atmosphere in which all participants can reflect and heal on their journey to the Vietnam Memorial in Washington D.C. in the hope that they can return home to a new beginning."[18] Today, Vietnam vets are aging and fewer in number, but veterans from more recent conflicts are starting to fill in. This annual motorcycle procession is unusual as far as US examples go in that the journey is equally or perhaps even more important than the ultimate destination.

Yet another set of possible new American pilgrimages could include mass gatherings of people to listen to music or to celebrate alternative lifestyles or expression. Music festivals such as Coachella in California, Summerfest in Wisconsin, and Bonnaroo in Tennessee have attracted large numbers of visitors on an annual basis. Journeys to these mass gatherings in the United States could be considered pilgrimage. They provide participants with time away from their everyday lives, an opportunity to be in community with friends and fellow fans, and to have spiritual experiences of sorts assisted perhaps by alcohol or other drugs.

The Burning Man Festival is a similar gathering. It began in the mid-1980s with a small group of friends in California. It currently attracts more than seventy thousand participants annually. People create a temporary city in the shape of a great arc in the Nevada desert and the gathering lasts for a week or more. Activities focus on creating art and experimenting with new forms of community and personal interactions. During the period of the festival, people dress in various costumes or dispense with clothes altogether, explore new roles for themselves, observe and make art, and of course participate in the ritual burning of a large wooden man. A number of temples have also been constructed in recent years. People post messages and leave memorabilia in such structures that is reminiscent of petitions for forgiveness and remembrance at traditional pilgrimage destinations—all of which also go up in flames at the end. The organizers' stated themes for the festival include notions such as a gift economy, decommodification, radical inclusion, communal effort and responsibility, and embodied participation. These sound oddly familiar and similar to many of the ideals often associated with pilgrimages!

ARE EXISTING PILGRIMAGE OPTIONS SUFFICIENT?

US society and culture apparently have changed and continue to evolve. There is a more diverse set of voices and belief systems, and religious sensibilities are certainly evolving in new ways. Unfortunately, the landscapes we inhabit are not well suited to either this growing diversity or this evolution in belief. People in the United States still live in landscapes and locales that are highly utilitarian and organized around capitalism, consumerism, and private property. Landscapes are treated more as commodities than as sacred or holy space. Changes to society and culture seem to be ahead of the ability of institutions, organized religions, or governments to provide the infrastructure of places and routes. The demand is growing rapidly, but the supply is yet to be delivered.

Catholic and Mormon destinations could continue to fulfill the need for many members of such populations. Places such as Sedona and Graceland have emerged to serve the pilgrimage needs of certain other groups. Even so, we might question whether all these existing options are anywhere near sufficient to meet the growing demand for a deep and rich pilgrimage experience for the many. While existing pilgrimage destinations might attract significant numbers of visitors, most people in the US continue to be left with few or no options. This is because current pilgrimage destinations are too far away, too expensive to get to, or perhaps because they are somehow less compelling if the individual is not Catholic or Mormon or does not share New Age beliefs or the adoration of a particular pop figure. It is true, for example, that Sedona has a wide appeal in terms of its scenic qualities, but fewer Americans are likely to truly believe in vortexes and energy fields. Graceland piques the curiosity of many, but the Presley homestead and tomb appeals on a deeper spiritual level to a narrower demographic in the United States.

This country still has a number of wilderness areas and other largely untouched natural areas. If these places are indeed sacred space and trips to them qualify as pilgrimage, then options for Americans remain somewhat broader. There is no doubt that a significant number of individuals walking the Appalachian or Pacific Crest trails are doing it as a kind of personal pilgrimage.

Counting on wilderness areas to meet the demand for pilgrimage experiences is problematic, however. Wilderness is an interpretation in many ways. For example, all wilderness areas are not equal in our perception of their being sacred. Untouched grasslands or thick swamps, despite being largely devoid of humans and human modifications on the landscape, are not usually thought of or treated as if they were sacred space or even worthy of aesthetic appreciation.[19] In the United States, sacred wilderness is more commonly thought of as dramatic mountain scenery with soaring peaks, alpine lakes, and rushing rivers. Natural spectacles such as the Grand Canyon and rugged coastlines make the grade, but vast stretches of boreal forests or the grasslands of the Great Plains, not so much.

Even for those who perceive wilderness to be sacred space, there is some question as to what degree trips to such areas are or even can be conducted in a pilgrimage-like manner. Most wilderness journeys today are primarily recreational experiences. Sometimes wilderness treks are simply ways of proving to yourself or others that you can physically walk or paddle the necessary distances. Certain activities and large communal gatherings are prohibited or regulated on federal or state lands. Elderly people and individuals with various disabilities find it difficult or impossible to navigate most wilderness trails. Wilderness might be perceived as sacred space, but Americans don't or can't always behave as if such tracts were sacred or that they are on a pilgrimage while there.

Building a stone cairn or stupa has become a popular outdoor activity and might be one exception. It is a way that hikers occasionally mark their presence in such places and perhaps commemorate a spiritual experience they had in the wild. Unfortunately, cairns are proliferating and in some cases are having a negative impact on the environment and prove distracting from the wilderness experience itself.[20]

Most US wilderness areas are far from major population centers. Becoming even more dependent on designated wilderness areas to serve the growing demand for pilgrimage would mean greater reliance on long-range transport, which is still largely based on fossil fuel consumption. Long-distance travel is costly and entails a great deal of environmental impact.

Thus, wilderness areas are not well suited to meet the growing demand for their use as pilgrimage destinations. Such areas can accommodate only small numbers of visitors at any given time in order to maintain their wilderness character. Americans should not depend on the wilderness areas to entirely meet the demand for pilgrimage or sacred space in the future because of the burden that places on people to travel to them, and the burden the places must bear as increased numbers of people tromp across and through them.

On the other hand, it could be just a matter of scale. Wilderness does not have to be hundreds or thousands of square miles. Natural places and pocket wildernesses could well be important components of any pilgrimage. If we could focus on smaller natural areas or features rather than expansive wilderness there are many more possibilities. Rural and even urban land-scapes can still provide pilgrims with contact with ecological communities, free-flowing streams, and wildlife—much of the otherness or connection pilgrims may be looking for.

A different set of concerns surround New Age and pop icon efforts at creating sacred space and pilgrimage. One common assertion is that such practices and pilgrimages are shallow and selfish. Critics contend that such pilgrims seem to be going to trendy places solely with the intent of having a pleasurable and perhaps pampered experience, something akin to going to a spa. They hope to come away energized and healthier, perhaps even glow-ing with a newly fueled and burnished aura. Some of the concerns of more traditional pilgrimages such as atonement for sins, dealing with your own death or that of loved ones, and deepening your own beliefs and faith might be given little or no attention. There seems to be no great emphasis in New Age or pop icon pilgrimage narratives about serving others or living a life of self-denial. Instead, these places and experiences can be seen as just another form of consumption in a late capitalist world.[21]

Others might say that some US pilgrimage practices today are yet another manifestation of social privilege in our society. Most of the people participating in pilgrimages are white and come from middle- to upper middle-class backgrounds. It takes a significant amount of time and money to participate in journeys, say to Sedona or Mount Shasta. Trips to overseas destinations are even more expensive and time consuming. Those who are less fortunate but might in fact also want to go on pilgrimage are denied the opportunity by circumstance and class.

Some attempts at creating new kinds of sacred space or practices have come under criticism because they appear to indiscriminately and inappropriately take from other religious traditions. Buddhist prayer flags, Hindu meditation and yoga, Taoist feng shui, and Wiccan rituals are common features or characteristics at places like Sedona or Mount Shasta. In particular, the widespread appropriation of Indigenous American practices and beliefs has come under scrutiny. European Americans have taken Indigenous American land, destroyed their communities, widely discriminated against them, and now in many ways seem to be trying to take over their religion and sacred places without deep understanding or permission. It is one thing to appreciate a religion or religious perspective different from your own. However, it is another thing altogether to cherry-pick rituals to participate in or to use images and symbols according to your own preferences and understanding. Indigenous Americans and others have understandably cried out against such practices, especially when non-natives use them for their own material gain. Non-natives swarming over Indigenous American sacred places without permission or deeper understanding can be especially appalling to Indigenous groups, even if non-natives do it with good intentions.

One dilemma that any pilgrimage shares with tourism is the possible impact on host communities. There is a large literature on this topic in tourism studies. It is not always clear as to how it relates to pilgrimage. Nevertheless, aspiring pilgrims should ask questions that have to do with the possible impacts of large or increased numbers of people traveling to a place on local populations and communities. There can be both positive and negative impacts on individuals and communities. What has the growth of pilgrims or tourists, for example, had on the people who lived in Sedona before the big increase in visitors? Are all the local people in northern California happy to see the large numbers of pilgrims to Mount Shasta? These are questions that any responsible pilgrim should be sensitive to.

In the same sense that new and increased pilgrimage activity might impact local communities, this also brings with it the potential for serious environmental impacts. Since a person undertaking any kind of pilgrimage in the United States today typically begins by getting in an automobile or an airplane, the carbon footprint and associated impacts of such pilgrimages can be significant. If three million pilgrims a year are driving hundreds or even thousands of miles to Sedona, imagine how much carbon and other pollutants are released into the atmosphere! Even low-impact wilderness treks typically involve a great deal of travel on freeways and backroads before the walking or paddling can commence.

Once pilgrims arrive at a destination, they might well require lodging and food. Destination locales often offer shopping opportunities and other services as well. Pilgrimage destinations located in sensitive ecological areas, such as alpine meadows, deserts, and wildlife reserves are especially vulnerable. Such ecosystems can be negatively impacted by large numbers of people, noise, and associated construction activities. Roadways and parking lots in any locale or environment create extensive impermeable surfaces that negatively affect streams and other water bodies.

Americans are known for their high consumption patterns. In addition to an automobile-based transportation system, they usually insist on having hot and cold running water and modern lodging facilities. They eat at restaurants and want to have nearby recreational activities. Large amounts of solid waste and wastewater can be generated. We should question the wisdom of this increasingly high-impact lifestyle anywhere in the US, but especially in places that we recognize or designate as sacred, spiritual, or holy.

CONCLUSION

People in the United States avoided creating or going on pilgrimages for centuries because of Protestant prohibitions and an embrace of Enlightenment rationality. Conditions and perceptions are changing, however. Based on demographic and cultural trends currently taking place in the United States, there is ample evidence of a real and growing need for additional and perhaps better opportunities to go on pilgrimage. Existing pilgrimages along with recently developed ones are inadequate or insufficient to meet the growing demand. Some of the pilgrimages that currently exist might also be culturally or environmentally inappropriate and ill-suited to growing social justice and sustainability concerns.

What is clearly needed are additional and new ways for greater numbers of Americans to participate in pilgrimage. These pilgrimages will need to be meaningful and appropriate to an increasingly diverse population and one that at least partially turns away from traditional religious models and beliefs. These pilgrimages need to minimize any possible associated social and environmental impacts.

Pilgrimage's Untapped Potential in the United States

Pilgrimage is typically thought of as a religious activity. A somewhat different way to approach the topic is from a humanistic perspective. Whatever it might entail from religious viewpoints, pilgrimage is also one of the most human activities we can do. Perhaps the gods have never really needed humans to go on pilgrimage, in any case. It is instead something that we ourselves need. To go on pilgrimage is inherent not so much to organized religion or doctrinal mandates, but intrinsic and central to what it means to be human.

If this is so, then a key justification for increasing the pilgrimage options available in the United States is not necessarily to bolster a specific established religion or denomination. It would not be a fundamentalist message that says we have strayed from some true path and need to get back to an imagined or ideal relationship with the divine. The reason to spend resources and time on developing new pilgrimage options in the United States today is simply to give Americans better opportunities to become deeper, more fulfilled individuals. Pilgrimages can facilitate the process of becoming a more humane and better person, no matter what that person's belief might be or even if they lack any religious convictions. Prophets and wise individuals throughout the ages have reminded us that humans do not live by bread alone. We also need to have experiences that feed our souls or deep human aspirations and longings. What people need today is the same as what humans for tens of thousands of years and in all traditions have needed: time away from our everyday lives, healing, atonement and forgiveness, spiritual encounters and transformation, time for reflection and the search for meaning, and opportunities to deeply connect with others.

Humans are half of this world and half not. We are a paradox. There is no doubt that as biological and material beings, we are bound to the earth and the larger cosmos in a thousand ways and in complex webs of relationship. From the moment we are born to the day we die, this is an inescapable fact. Although extreme materialists and even some religious traditions deny that we are anything other than this, most maintain that we are indeed more. Something different. Humans are not really *apart from* but not entirely *of* the physical world either, at least as we understand it today. Loren Eiseley wrote that there came a point in human evolution when "for the first time in four billion years a living creature had contemplated himself and heard with a sudden, unaccountable loneliness, the whisper of the wind in the night reeds."[1]

As an embodied ritual, pilgrimage speaks to humans as both biological and spiritual beings. Pilgrimage is nothing if not an intense physical activity. It is the movement of our bodies through space. It involves a rich tapestry of sights, sounds, smells, tastes, and touch. And yet it is also about the other side of our nature—that which we might call spirit or soul—whatever it is that is not entirely reducible to our material existence. People's lives can become unbalanced or they can become literally ill when one side or the other dominates. Such a condition denies our humanity, and Americans have in many ways been denied the benefits of pilgrimage in this regard for most of our history.

If the United States could figure out how to support and sensitively develop new pilgrimages, a number of benefits should accrue. There is already ample evidence that pilgrimage can be good for individuals. I contend that increased pilgrimage activity also has the potential to be highly beneficial for community building and creating a greener and more sustainable world.

PILGRIMAGE CAN BE GOOD FOR INDIVIDUALS

Pilgrimage has obviously appealed to humans throughout the ages and around the world, but in what sense can we say that pilgrimage is actually beneficial for individuals? At first glance, this wouldn't necessarily seem to be true. Some pilgrims have suffered from the hardships they endured on pilgrimage. Many spent a large portion of their limited financial resources. Perhaps some were coerced and indoctrinated into rituals that they didn't necessarily seek out or wish for themselves. While such possibilities exist, most pilgrims don't seem to focus on such matters. Instead they attest to the great fulfillment, joy, and benefits they received from their pilgrimage. They would encourage others to undertake their own journeys. For many individuals of all historical periods and traditions, their pilgrimage experience was not so much an ordeal but was rather one of the most positive and meaningful experiences of their lives.

One of the most commonly reported personal benefits of pilgrimage is healing. The literature on pilgrimage is full of such testimonials. Pilgrims throughout history have undertaken their journeys with the hope and expectation that they themselves or perhaps a loved one would be healed because of their journey. There are countless stories of pilgrims being cured of one physical ailment or another. Crutches left behind by pilgrims who hobbled to places such as Chimayó or Lourdes but then walked away healed attest to such claims. Before the advent of modern medicine, many saw pilgrimage as perhaps their best chance to ease their physical suffering. Nowadays, petitions for miraculous cures of physical ailments are not as prevalent. Clerics of the Catholic Church are careful to tone down such expectations at many shrines and pilgrimage destinations today. Many pilgrims are themselves simply reluctant to believe in miracles or that which defies scientific understanding and explanation. People in the modern world are less likely to hope for divine intervention and more likely to turn to the medical establishment for cures if they are available.

Although fewer people today expect that pilgrimage will help the lame to walk again or the sick to be cured of cancer or other diseases, many nevertheless continue to seek healing. The healing they seek is somewhat different than a strict medical cure. Healing has a number of other connotations. People suffer not only from physical afflictions, but psychological, social, and perhaps spiritual ones as well. Physical ailments are often related to or exacerbated by a person's state of mind or spiritual angst. Healing has an entirely different meaning in this regard.

There are many accounts of healing associated with pilgrimage in the world today. The Run for the Wall motorcycle pilgrimage is focused on healing the psychological trauma many Vietnam War vets experienced. Messages left at the Burning Man festival ask for healing of various psychological and spiritual ailments. There were even singular pilgrimage destinations in South Asia that attracted pilgrims from different religions including Islam, Hinduism, and Christianity.[2] The appeal of such shrines was that their reputation for healing, and the prospect of being healed apparently overrode any doctrinal differences for many pilgrims. The pilgrimage destination at Sainte-Anne-de-Beaupré in Quebec has been described as being a "therapeutic landscape,"[3] a term coined in an earlier study focusing on Lourdes and other locations.[4] Jill Dubisch and Michael Winkelman write, in their introduction to their book on pilgrimage and healing:

> *Pilgrimage is a "multimedia therapy" that combines many different kinds of healing processes that are not normally found within a single healing tradition or activity. It is a form of "biopsychosocial" and spiritual healing that addresses many levels of the human need for healing and "wholing" the person.[5]*

One of the more fascinating examples of such healing in the modern world centers around a joint Netherlands program uniting several pilgrimage organizations and health insurance companies that facilitated a pilgrimage to Lourdes for sick and elderly citizens. Dutch health insurance companies actually paid for nearly two thousand individuals a year to go to Lourdes, accompanied by doctors and nurses. Although there was some debate about the ethics and efficacy of this, the program seemed to be quite successful. Dutch society has become highly secular, and Catholics also have long been a marginalized minority in this historically Protestant country. These pilgrimages did not necessarily directly cure their physical ailments, but did succeed in giving pilgrims a way to express their pain and deal with their feelings of loss. This program proved highly therapeutic, and these elderly Catholic pilgrims experienced improvements in their overall health and well-being.[6]

Could such a program happen in the United States? It is hard to imagine Medicare or any other US health insurance entity agreeing to such an arrangement. Something like this program might eventually happen, but not until health and healing are looked at in a more holistic sense, and meaningful pilgrimage destinations are more readily available nearby.

Instead of healing per se, walking pilgrimages can have other direct health and wellness benefits for individuals. Walking a pilgrimage can simply be good exercise and a way to get into better physical shape. Walking as wellness can be more than that, however. Pilgrimage can make people become more at ease in their own bodies. It can create a balance lacking in the modern world. Many studies in the last few years have extolled the health and wellness benefits of walking.

Many of today's pilgrimages in Japan are promoted as exercises in holistic healing and health. They don't ignore the religious and spiritual dimensions, but the idea of *iyashi,* which refers to general physical and mental restoration, seems to have much appeal as well.[7] Many of the pilgrimages around Kumano, a region with a number of ancient pilgrimage routes, have a network of geo-therapists who are trained to facilitate activities that promote such holistic healing. They will often walk with pilgrims. They also encourage or provide healthy food, mountain herbs, use of silence, and other such techniques to promote overall well-being.

One of the other most common goals of pilgrims throughout the ages has not been healing per se, but rather the seeking of forgiveness and atonement. People often feel that they need to atone and be forgiven before any healing can occur. They realize and regret the fact that they sinned in some fashion, failed to communicate with or help others in need, or took some other action or inaction that was hurtful or caused pain or injury. Many people now are even considering making atonement for sins they might have committed against the earth itself! Whatever the cause, humans around the world suffer regularly and often intensely from feelings of guilt. Whether the individual feels they have sinned against their god or another human being or perhaps the planet, pilgrimage seems to be a way for people to acknowledge their transgressions and ask for forgiveness, as well as to seek atonement.

If their transgression was against another person, it could be that the person is now dead or gone from their lives or is simply unwilling or unable to accept such pleas directly. People are thus left with few options. If their sin is against their god, then perhaps traveling to a sacred place is where they feel their prayers can be heard most effectively and the divine presence can attest to their sincerity by their actions. Many individuals in the past and even today purposely make pilgrimage into an act of atonement by various actions including prostrating themselves or traversing long distances on their knees, afflicting pain upon themselves in other ways, or undertaking various austerities. The Catholic pilgrims at St. Patrick's Purgatory in Ireland remain barefoot in the cold and go without food and sleep for long periods. Pilgrims on the *Arba'een* pilgrimage to Karbala, Iraq, often suffer from the heat and long distances as a means of atonement. Pilgrims attest to the effectiveness of such pleas for forgiveness and acts of atonement. They return home with some sense of closure and a lightening of their burden. Their feelings of guilt are diminished or transformed.

Another important reason pilgrimage can be good for individuals is that many feel the need to simply give thanks to their god, the universe, or certain other individuals. Sometimes just articulating thanks is not enough. The opportunity to spend days or weeks in vigorous travel acknowledging the gift of life, love, or good fortune can be highly therapeutic and meaningful. We have all been given many gifts in our lives. Pilgrimage can be an especially effective way to express thanks. Most religions encourage their adherents to give thanks and acknowledge the debt they owe for all that has been given to them.

Pilgrimage can be beneficial for individuals in that it simply provides an opportunity to have time out and time away from their everyday lives. Abrahamic traditions set aside a Sabbath. Even in secular settings, there is a deeply ingrained sense that people need a break from their routines in order to remain healthy and happy individuals. Humans benefit in any number of ways by being away from their daily responsibilities and routines from time to time. For many in a secular society, this simply means a weekend getaway or an annual vacation. A few employers today are encouraging, and in some cases even paying, their employees to take several weeks to a month off to travel. They expect that their employees will come back energized, healthier, and better able to contribute creatively to the organization. The sabbatical has long been institutionalized in higher education and for members of the clergy in various denominations. Sabbaths, sabbaticals, and pilgrimages are not ways of escaping responsibilities, or opportunities for being lazy. They are occasions to undertake that which the individual feels is necessary or compelling but which is not possible to accomplish in the normal course of affairs.

From a religious perspective, pilgrimage is an opportunity to revive and reinvigorate your spiritual life and to replenish your soul in a way that is not normally possible. Pilgrimage provides not only a break from the everyday but also an opportunity to be in both liminal time and liminal space—sacred time and sacred place. Pilgrims often attest to the power of pilgrimage to put them in a deeply introspective or even otherworldly state of mind and behavior. It can be a powerful and transformative spiritual experience.[8]

Many people use pilgrimage as a time to mark transitions and rites of passage in their own lives. Coming of age, completing an education or training, moving, getting married or divorced, starting or losing a job, or beginning retirement at the end of a long working career are all important life transitions. Modern societies and even religious organizations are not often successful at creating rituals and activities that help individuals make such dramatic changes in their lives and social status. Many pilgrims today are taking their journeys at precisely such moments and find it a more satisfying way to ritually mark and commemorate junctures in their lives.

Pilgrimage can be particularly important when dealing with death, perhaps humankind's most profound transition. This might be either an individual's own eventuality or the more immediate loss of a loved one. The central theme of the popular film entitled *The Way*,[9] written, directed, and produced by Emilio Estevez and starring Martin Sheen, deals with this explicitly. The main character has an adult son who is struck by lightning and dies just as he is beginning his pilgrimage on the *Camino de Santiago*. The father comes from the US to claim the body and has his son cremated in the French village near where he was killed. The father, who had been quite skeptical of his son's endeavor, nevertheless decides to stay and complete the pilgrimage in his son's stead. He chooses to leave his son's ashes at various locations along the way. In the process, the father is able to truly mourn, seek atonement for his troubled relationship with his son, and be healed. Similarly, in the novel by Rachel Joyce, *The Unlikely Pilgrimage of Harold Fry*, the main character hastily begins a journey, ostensibly to visit an old colleague who is dying. In the course of his unlikely walking pilgrimage all the way across England, he ends up dealing with a tragic death in his own family, something he found impossible to do previously.[10]

Death is a major theme in the *Henro*. The traditional clothing for Japanese pilgrims in Shikoku is all white, denoting that during the course of the pilgrimage, they are dead to the world or ready for their own death—whenever that may come. A number of stops along the way are tomb sites, cemeteries, and other places for the dead. Mountains in general have been perceived by the Japanese as places of the spirits of the deceased. Many believe that spirits still inhabit such locales. Pilgrims can come to grips with their own death by praying and meditating in such places. Some pilgrims carry ashes or photographs of lost loved ones.

Millions of Hindus regularly travel to the city of Banaras. Many go only to bathe in the sacred waters and participate in other rituals. Others go there to die or at least have their remains cast into the river. Diana Eck writes, "Here the smoke of the cremation pyres rises heavenward with the spires of a hundred temples and the ashes of the dead swirl through the waters of the Ganges, the river of life."[11] Death is a central and compelling theme in any pilgrimage to Banaras, one of the largest in terms of number of pilgrims and one of the oldest in terms of longevity.

PILGRIMAGE CAN BE GOOD FOR COMMUNITY

Pilgrimage can be good for community as well as for individuals. Many commentators on the United States today talk about a more dysfunctional, less communitarian society. Our political discourse has become increasingly strident and polarized. We know the characters in movies and TV shows better than we know our neighbors. People have more acquaintances and social media contacts but fewer close friends. Extended families are rare as grown children move away and their families often end up scattered across the country. Lower fertility rates result in fewer siblings, cousins, and aunts and uncles. Mental illness and depression seem to afflict larger and larger portions of our society. Social capital is perhaps at an all-time low and people are not even "bowling alone."[12] They are simply staying home, are on social media, and are increasingly isolated.

Since the first experimental model communities were created in Britain as an alternative to the horrific conditions of industrial cities of the nineteenth century, urban planners have been trying to create cities that better cater to our social selves. They have rarely been successful. The modernist architecture and urban renewal of the 1950s and 1960s often ended disastrously. The Pruitt-Igoe housing development in St. Louis began to decline within a few years of construction and had to be completely demolished around twenty years after it was built. The low-density sprawl that characterizes most US cities today was marginally better, but few, if any, still celebrate its communitarian qualities.[13] New urbanism and "smart growth" urban planning models focus to a large degree on improving the social climate of urban areas, but areas so transformed are limited in extent and success is difficult to measure as of yet. Since the vast majority of Americans today live in urban areas, we might conclude that the places most Americans live in remain alienating and difficult places to foster real community. Shopping malls and online purchasing have not successfully replaced Main Street, at least in communitarian terms.

We are also living in an increasingly diverse society. This is a positive development, but for some it is an ongoing struggle. As was noted earlier, the United States is certainly more diverse in terms of our religious identification. America is no longer predominantly Protestant, although Protestants of various denominations remain major voices in the choir. Now those who claim no religion at all—along with Hindu, Buddhist, Muslim, and others— are changing and expanding the chorus. Immigration has broadened US society to include larger numbers of people from Latin America, Asia, and elsewhere across the globe. In many urban areas, languages from around the world can be heard on the streets, in schools, and in businesses. Mosques, Hindu temples, and Buddhist stupas are rising up next to churches and synagogues.

While such diversity can be a positive force in social evolution, it can also result in reactionary responses of hate, fear, and even violence. The experiences of African Americans, Indigenous Americans, Latinx Americans, Asian Americans, and now Muslim Americans offer ample evidence of such negative responses. There is a great need in our society today to better celebrate our diverse ethnic, racial, and religious communities. There is no stopping the forces of the modern world and certainly no reason to do so. Human cultural diversity and a pluralistic society are to be welcomed and embraced. How best to do this is not easy to determine. Issues of class, privilege, and a history of discrimination and violence are woven deeply into the narrative.

Pilgrimage is no panacea, but it could be part of the solution to both the concerns about an increasing lack of social interaction and the challenges of an increasingly diverse society. More people going on more and increasingly diverse pilgrimages can potentially help weave more positive communities that heal the pain of isolation and the evils of discrimination and privilege. All humans have a need to belong. We are born entirely dependent on others, and to a degree we never lose such dependency. As Larry Rasmussen points out, we are "born to belonging"[14] and alone incapable of producing even a #2 pencil. It takes a community. How then can pilgrimage support such community building and reinforcement?

What has been true for pilgrimages around the world and throughout history is that most pilgrims go on their journeys with others. They travel with family members or people from their own village or parish. They go with members of their own congregations or at least their own denominations. The experience becomes de facto a communal experience. Hardships endured become shared hardships, and moments of bliss are not entirely otherworldly.

In the United States today such practices and patterns could certainly continue. Families might want to go on pilgrimage together as a way of not only reinforcing their beliefs or searching for the divine, but also as a way to be together and strengthen familial bonds as they seek healing and enlightenment. Sally Welch, an Anglican cleric, has eloquently spoken about the importance of pilgrimages she has taken with members of her family.[15] Clubs and organizations might decide to do pilgrimages together for all the personal reasons individuals go on pilgrimage, but also to develop group trust and build a solid team identity. Friends and perhaps even work-affiliated groups could do so for similar reasons.

There is a long history of denominational groups and members of congregations going on pilgrimage together. Such outings have the potential for not only individual transformation, but also for the strengthening of bonds and commitment to the congregation and faith tradition. Such experiences would have dividends for the group for years and even lifetimes. This can occur on the immediate and local level as well as the global. One of the purposes of the *Hajj* is to create a global sense of community among Muslims of all ethnicities, languages, and citizenships. At the same time, self-identified and locally formed groups on the *Hajj* can celebrate their own particular group's experience as it is integrated and interwoven into the larger whole.

An innovative pilgrimage in Kyoto, Japan, encourages older citizens to walk various pilgrimage routes through the city. The purpose is as much to create community as it is to promote more spiritual concerns. Older citizens walk in large part as a kind of neighborhood watch to make sure schoolchildren are safe on their journeys to and from school. These elder pilgrims take circuitous paths to various statues of the bodhisattva Jizo, who is associated with watching over children. This whole exercise helps connect older and younger generations and provides older citizens of the city with greater purpose and community.[16]

Pilgrimages can also strengthen local communities simply in their creation and maintenance, if done in a communitarian way. Common ownership of a resource has often been the glue that helps bind members of a community together. All members have a stake and are accountable to each other. If the creation of new pilgrimages is done in such a way, all or most members of a locality could feel some pride of ownership and a sense of common purpose.

If such community building could be thought of as building fences to define and strengthen groups, then the parallel task is to reach out to the wider world by installing gates in these metaphorical fences. This too, is an area where a newly conceived pilgrimage model or tradition might help. Pilgrimage is a way for individuals to seek personal healing, but it also might be a way to heal the larger culture and society. Pilgrimage can be an innovative way to strengthen understanding and promote social justice.

One way to accomplish this is to incorporate service into pilgrimage. There is no reason why some pilgrims couldn't include service activities into their experience, just as many tourists and students do while visiting or studying abroad. The ways in which this might happen are limited only by a pilgrim's imagination. Perhaps pilgrimage could copy the model of walk-a-thons by getting sponsors in order to raise money for various charitable causes. Perhaps there could be sites along the way where pilgrims could volunteer their time and skills. Their service might be to help those with disabilities or financial constraints to be able to participate in the pilgrimage.

Another way to heal the larger society is simply to locate pilgrimage routes in areas that are suffering economically. Pilgrims could help support local economies in such areas as they would have a need for lodging, food, and other services. Like tourism, pilgrimage could be an effective way to transfer wealth and create greater economic equality and opportunity. Locating new pilgrimage routes in areas with declining populations might help slow or perhaps even reverse that decline.

A significant way to open these metaphorical gates is to develop interfaith pilgrimages. One method for accomplishing this is to incorporate religiously diverse destinations along one pilgrimage route. Pilgrims on the *Henro* stop at eighty-eight Buddhist temples as they traverse the island of Shikoku. Why not have a US pilgrimage that has numerous stops and includes not only Buddhist temples, but also Christian churches, Islamic mosques, Hindu temples, or perhaps even sacred springs or groves? Many individuals in the United States today, especially those who might see themselves as spiritual but not religious, could embrace such an experience. Done in a sensitive manner, even pilgrims that adhere to one faith could return home with not only a better understanding of their own beliefs, but appreciation and deeper understanding of other traditions as well.

A second way to accomplish an inter-religious experience would be to form groups of pilgrims of different beliefs or traditions. They would simply journey together. The conversations could be many and wide ranging. This kind of learning could be enlightening as long as the individuals were able to listen deeply—not necessarily to be converted to one point of view or another—but simply to understand and appreciate the differences and similarities involved.

Pilgrimage could also do much to encourage pilgrims to be more aware of social justice. Pilgrimage routes could be designed in such a way as to allow pilgrims to experience firsthand the social realities and injustices of the world we live in. For example, a pilgrimage route could traverse distinct neighborhoods or regions of various ethnicities, race, and incomes. Many people are unaware even of what certain neighborhoods in their own cities look like. Imagine walking from the richest neighborhood to the poorest in any metro area of the country—the contrasts would be striking. Imagine going from neighborhoods that are almost entirely white to those almost entirely African American or Latinx. This could inspire pilgrims to work for social justice throughout their lives. Of course, such treks should be done carefully and with permission of the communities involved. One way to ensure this would be to create opportunities to meet residents, and hear their perspectives and concerns about their own neighborhoods. Pilgrims could perhaps contribute financially to neighborhood projects in low-income areas or take advantage of service opportunities.

Pilgrimage routes might similarly include stops at places where civil rights struggles and significant events in the history of social justice and equality have played out. Why couldn't some pilgrimages include stops or destinations such as Selma, Alabama; the Stonewall Inn in New York; Japanese internment camps in the west; or Seneca Falls in upstate New York? Such places call out for greater understanding and inclusivity. If not sacred space, such locales are certainly "redolent with meaning."[17]

There is a great deal of environmental injustice in the United States. Some pilgrimages could make participants better aware of such situations. Pilgrimages might, for example, go downwind or downstream from major pollution sources. Pilgrims could personally witness the impact such pollution has on people most affected by it. Pilgrimage routes could wind through neighborhoods torn apart by freeway construction or disrupted by unwanted gentrification. Pilgrimage routes that skirt Superfund sites or mining scars would render the invisible more visible. They could also make pilgrims aware of the communities where such features are located, as well as the residents who necessarily have to cope with the presence of such dangers every day.

PILGRIMAGE AS A WAY TO IMPROVE THE ENVIRONMENT AND CREATE A MORE SUSTAINABLE WORLD

The potential of new pilgrimage routes extends even further. As explored above, increased pilgrimage activity and a greater selection of pilgrimage options could potentially heal individuals, communities, and cultures in the US. They could also help heal Planet Earth.

Most pilgrimages in the past or even today are not environmentally friendly. That was never their intention. Some, in fact, have dramatic environmental impacts. Thousands of people traveling many miles in airplanes and cars and converging on a particular location can create serious problems in terms of carbon emissions, water pollution, waste disposal, impacts on vegetation and soils, and so forth. Traditional pilgrimages in nearly all religious traditions have historically been more focused on what were considered otherworldly concerns such as encounters and communication with the divine, spiritual awakening, or bonding with fellow pilgrims. Concerns about climate change, water pollution, proliferation of impervious surfaces, declining air quality, loss of the earth's biodiversity, and other related topics were not high priorities. Such concerns are all relatively new in most non-Indigenous cultures and certainly most religious traditions. Few pilgrims in the past have ventured forth with the specific intent to save the planet.

Saving the planet, however, is increasingly becoming a pressing concern around the world and in many religious traditions as well. Organized religions previously might have been relatively slow to move in this direction, but today most are doing exactly that and are increasingly becoming a significant force for environmentalism in the world. Theologians and lay people across the religious spectrum are forging ahead with reimagined cosmologies and the formulation of religiously inspired environmental ethics. Many interfaith dialogues and conferences focus on shared environmental concerns. The greening of Christianity, Islam, Judaism, Buddhism, and others is in full force across the globe. Indeed, the fact that Pope Francis has produced a lengthy encyclical letter[18] on care for our common home with an emphasis on climate change underscores the transformations now taking place even at the highest levels.

Pilgrimage, as part of this awakening, can be reenvisioned to assure a greener and more sustainable world in the future. There is a Green Pilgrimage Network, a collaboration between more than twenty-five cities and pilgrimage destination sites.[19] Participating pilgrimages are finding innovative ways to reduce environmental impacts. A film entitled *Pad Yatra: A Green Odyssey*[20] documented a 450-mile pilgrimage that took place in 2013, with 700 pilgrims. They made an arduous trek through the Himalayas that highlighted the environmental problems of the region and included educational and service components. Pilgrims picked up literally tons of high-altitude trash along the way.

Pilgrimage can help heal Planet Earth in at least two different ways. Going on pilgrimage can, first of all, facilitate the process of changing people's attitudes, beliefs, and behaviors. Pilgrims might be encouraged to behave in a certain way, such as cleaning up along the route or reducing their own consumption. Their attention might also be directed to the sacred qualities of the environment they visit, and they might thereby see the world through a new lens. Secondly, pilgrimage routes and infrastructure can be designed or modified to create actual physical changes on the landscape.

What are some of the design features and changes to infrastructure that might be employed? There are many possibilities, and pilgrimage planners undoubtedly can be creative and innovative if given the opportunity. A key aspect is reducing fossil fuel consumption. This means new pilgrimages should be created in such a way that mobility focuses more on walking and less on motorized vehicles. Buildings and structures that cater to pilgrims such as hostels, inns, and restaurants could be built mostly out of local materials and be energy efficient—perhaps relying entirely on renewable energy sources. Impervious surfaces would be limited or remediated to deal with runoff from rooftops and paved areas. Water consumption at places where pilgrims congregate or stay overnight should be minimized, especially in arid regions. Sewage from hotels, hostels, food services, and bathroom facilities should be thoroughly treated to prevent any pollution of surface or groundwater. Use of herbicides, pesticides, and other toxic chemicals could be limited or avoided altogether.

One of the most vexing US environmental problems today is our loss of biodiversity. Large numbers of plant and animal species are threatened, endangered, or their populations are being dramatically reduced. One of the main reasons is that natural habitats have been destroyed as Americans continue to convert forests, wetlands, prairies, and other ecosystems into office parks, subdivisions, retail malls, lawns, parking lots, roads, and other land uses. A serious aspect of habitat loss is not simply an overall reduction of area, but a fragmentation as well. In other words, there might be a patch of forest here and a patch of forest there, but birds and animals are not able to easily get from one patch of habitat to another. Plants and animals can become isolated. Various species could experience population declines and lose genetic diversity.

Pilgrimage routes that are sensitively and carefully designed could help. Reconciliation or "Win-Win Ecology"[21] asserts that the future of biodiversity and wildlife conservation is not so much in preservation of large tracts of wilderness, but in making suitable habitats for plants and animals amidst the human landscapes of the world. Wildlife experts, botanists, and ecologists could be enlisted to help plan and develop pilgrimage routes also serving as effective corridors for wildlife and plant movement and dispersal. Pilgrimage routes could simultaneously increase and connect habitats for flora and fauna while serving the spiritual and emotional needs of human pilgrims. Imagine, for example, a monarch butterfly pilgrimage route, with miles of milkweed and nectar providing flowers. Such a route could be one way to truly make atonement to the planet.

There is at least one major trail effort of this sort already taking place. The Algonquin to Adirondacks Collaborative, also known as the A2A,[22] is working to create an approximately four-hundred-mile trail leading from the heart of the Adirondacks in upstate New York to Algonquin Provincial Park in Ontario. While their main stated purpose is to create a wildlife corridor, they are also interested in promoting a walking trail that serves a number of human needs and desires. Some of the members of the collaborative explicitly cite the *Camino de Santiago* as an inspiration and model,[23] and hope that pilgrims as well as animals will eventually traverse the route.

An additional way to expand natural habitats in conjunction with pilgrimage routes is to incorporate green cemeteries. Green cemeteries are places where the dead are buried, but only in eco-friendly wooden boxes, baskets, or pods that will decompose. Bodies are not treated with toxic chemicals before burial. People who choose to be cremated can also have their ashes located in such cemeteries. Green cemeteries themselves are not groomed as lawns or parklike settings, but remain as natural ecosystems: prairies, forests, or whatever is native for the region. Creating a hundred-acre cemetery, for example, would be the functional equivalent of preserving and protecting a hundred-acre natural ecosystem.

In early US history, most Americans were Christians, and most Christians wanted to be buried as close as possible to a church. The church was seen as a gateway to heaven. Such literal heaven and hell cosmology is less prevalent in current religion in America. Instead, Christians and others are increasingly looking to natural places even beyond the typical garden cemeteries to have their remains placed after they die. Natural places are already or increasingly seen as sacred space for many.

Places for the dead inherently fit well with pilgrimage routes, since places for the dead usually in themselves create a sense of the numinous. Being able to contemplate your own or others' mortality by being in a green cemetery seems to resonate with many Americans today. Our cosmologies increasingly see the cycles and interactions of ecosystems as being central to our own notions of life and death.

The other way pilgrimage, apart from such physical changes and designs, could create a greener and more sustainable world is that the routes and process could be orchestrated in ways that might alter the behavior, attitudes, perceptions, and ethics of pilgrims. One way to affect pilgrims directly is to create pilgrimages that somehow focus their attention on the sacred or holy dimensions of the environment itself. Shrines and architecture have long been a "focusing lens"[24] for pilgrims. The challenge now is to extend the notion of the sacred beyond the confines of the temple and garden and in so doing create pilgrimages that actually enhance the pilgrim's environmental understanding, attitudes, and ethics.

Going on pilgrimage could strengthen the perception that Earth itself can be holy. The world is more than we know. People are increasingly changing their understanding and interpretation of their surroundings. Animals are increasingly thought to be not automatons, but rather sentient life forms with certain qualities and even rights. We think of the environment less as a collection of things and more as an integrated web of being and connection. People in the US today less often assert absolute dominion over plants and animals. Property rights are increasingly seen as entailing environmental responsibilities as well.

One of the main reasons people went on pilgrimage in the past is that it allowed them an opportunity to grieve. What they grieved for has typically been the loss of a loved one or perhaps a decline in their own health and well-being. There is now a growing perception and recognition that we also need to grieve environmental loss and degradation. Without proper recognition and attention to the emotional harm and deep losses we have already experienced, we are less able to move forward and deal with ongoing challenges. As with the loss of loved ones, we need a way to grapple with the full impact and ways to properly grieve the ecological losses that mount every day. Douglas Burton-Christie writes:

It is worth considering whether something like the practice of pethos, the cultivation of tears, can help us rekindle our awareness of the beauty and fragility of our shared life within the natural world, and in the process help us deepen our sense of responsibility and care for the world.[25]

CONCLUSION

There are compelling reasons why creating new pilgrimages and pilgrimage pathways for the United States have the potential for personal, social, and environmental benefits. We can learn a great deal from other parts of the world and from other historical periods about the reasons people participated in pilgrimages. Many of these same benefits should also be available to US residents today.

More importantly, we can also create pilgrimages that go beyond. We can create pilgrimages that not only heal and benefit individuals, but those that will help us create healthier communities and a more sustainable Earth.

5

Pathway, Spirit, and Place

There are additional considerations useful to ponder before the actual planning and creating pathways can begin. These concepts better define the parameters of what pilgrimage pathways in the United States might look like and accomplish.

PATHWAY VERSUS DESTINATION

Pilgrimage is most often conceived of as a journey to a sacred place, with both journey and destination being significant. Although both are usually necessary, the pilgrimage destination has often been given precedence over the journey—either by pilgrims themselves or by people who write about and try to understand pilgrimage. Historically, the priority given the destination may have been most common. For example, if medieval Christians in Europe had somehow been given the choice of getting on an airplane to Jerusalem or a fast train to Rome, they would most likely have done so. The route had little positive significance. It is telling that some individuals were sentenced by authorities to go on a long pilgrimage as a kind of penance or atonement for a sin or crime. The pilgrim's journey was assumed to be an ordeal. In medieval Europe and elsewhere in earlier times, pilgrims faced various hardships along the way, including hostile communities, criminals, disease, lack of food and water, inclement weather, and other obstacles in addition to the physical rigors of the walk itself.

On the other hand, with some pilgrimages, the journey itself has been especially significant and meaningful. Pilgrims have sometimes chosen to purposely make the journey difficult and challenging. At many Christian shrines, pilgrims complete a portion or all of their journey on their knees. Some of the Buddhist and Bon pilgrims at Mount Kailash in Tibet will prostrate themselves continuously as they go around the mountain. Other pilgrims have been known to inflict various injuries upon themselves as an act of penance and purposeful suffering along their route.

Nevertheless, in the modern world most pilgrims still try to minimize the difficulties and rigors of the journey, opt for the easiest and quickest way to get to their destination, and generally downplay the importance of the journey. Ian Reader notes that the majority of pilgrims on the *Henro* in the past several decades have made the journey by bus, and in some cases by private car and even helicopter. Most undertaking the *Hajj* today will fly to Jedda. Improvements in transportation make it much easier for Hindu pilgrims to travel to the *Char Dham*, or the four abodes—Badrinath in the north, Puri in the east, Rameswaram in the south, and Dwaraka in the west of India—in a relatively short time by traveling in buses or cars instead of walking these great distances across the subcontinent. Very few individuals in Europe today will walk a long distance to get to Lourdes or Fatima and will instead arrive by train, bus, or automobile.

This emphasis on destination might be changing, though. In the modern world of hypermobility and fast-paced lifestyles, many other pilgrims today are seeking to purposely slow things down. On certain pilgrimages, it seems that the journey itself has already or is quickly becoming the more important aspect. The purpose of walking a pilgrimage route in the modern world is less about suffering, and more about the positive aspects of the journey. The *Camino* might be the premier example of a renewed emphasis on the journey. An increasing number of Japanese and pilgrims from other parts of the world are spurning motorized transport and once again walking to the eighty-eight temples of the *Henro* as well.

Pilgrimage destinations typically have symbolic significance, whether a shrine, icon, mountain peak, or some type of sacred architecture. While traversing the route might have some significance as a ritual action or performance, it has historically been less significant in symbolic terms. Again, this seems to be changing. Interestingly, pilgrims today who choose to walk the *Henro* tend to see the temples as less important than do bus pilgrims, and the journey itself is instead what is most meaningful and transformative. This is also true of the Way of St. James. Walkers on the *Camino* today often skip altogether the visit to the cathedral at the end of the walk. The totality of landscape or multiple facets might be perceived as the purpose of a journey, with its own set of meanings and significance. Walking pilgrimages with no particular destination at all have become popular for Lutherans in Sweden.

The pilgrim destination has lost its significance as a holy place, and has a value primarily as a physical goal. Holy places are rather perceived and defined along the trail by the pilgrims individually. The setting— outdoor life and nature—now serves as an instrument for spiritual experiences.[1]

Because US residents do not widely share religious beliefs, it makes sense to think that new pilgrimage pathways might be better if they focused on the journey rather than the destination. It is hard to imagine a shrine, temple, or even a natural feature that would be conceived as a legitimate pilgrimage destination by even a majority of Americans. On the other hand, a journey, especially a walking journey, is something that everyone can relate to.

PATHWAY CONFIGURATIONS

How might these new pilgrimage routes be configured? Should the routes be defined or left up to the pilgrims themselves? Since the US has virtually no dedicated pilgrimage pathways, we might do well to see how other pilgrimages around the world are configured.

The annual Hindu pilgrimage from Sri Mahamariamman Temple in the center of Kuala Lumpur to the Batu Caves in Malaysia traverses a well-defined, fifteen-kilometer route each year during the Thaipusam Festival, for example. Other pilgrimages do not specify a route, and pilgrims can arrive at the destination from any direction and by any mode. In the case of the *Hajj*, it doesn't really matter how pilgrims get to Mecca, but once there, a highly specified and orchestrated route is expected as they go to locations such as the Plain of Arafat, Mina, and Muzdalifah. The *Henro* has fairly specified routes between the eighty-eight temples, but pilgrims have the option of starting at any point or going clockwise and counterclockwise—although it turns out that most pilgrims choose to begin and end at the same place and go in the same direction. Pilgrims can choose from several different routes to get to the Cathedral of Santiago de Compostela, but the number of official routes is limited to just a few. Buddhist pilgrims to the Perfume Pagoda in Vietnam all start at Ben Duc village by boarding a boat and then being rowed by local workers for several hours up the river. Pilgrims then walk or take a cable car to a cave and other destinations deep in the rugged karst topography. Christians in Jerusalem will walk the *Via Dolorosa*, the route that Jesus is said to have taken while carrying his own cross. In short, there is a great variation in routes and specificity of pathways associated with pilgrimages around the world. There really isn't a right or wrong way to configure a route. However, if the route is to be the main focus, then US pilgrimage planners will most likely want to limit the route to a single path to best achieve the aims of the walk.

The length of the journey also varies considerably. Some pilgrimages are relatively short and can be completed in a matter of hours or a day or two. Others involve great distances and time commitments to complete. In modern times, pilgrimages that previously involved long journeys for most pilgrims have largely been shortened by modern transportation systems. People now might travel hundreds or even thousands of miles, but do so on airplanes and in high-speed motorized vehicles. Often, pilgrims are asked to walk only the distances from the bus stop or nearby lodging to the actual shrine or focus of the pilgrimage.

In earlier times, any journey to a pilgrimage destination would also mean that once activities at the destination were complete, the pilgrim would then retrace their route to return home. Even though it was the same route, the meaning and significance might be diminished on the return trip. Participants in Pilgrimage groups in the Cuzco region of the Andes, and more specifically in Michael Sallnow's account of the pilgrimage to Qoyllur Rit'i, were more lackadaisical on the return trip to their villages than on the more scripted journey to the shrine.[2] Nowadays pilgrims typically do not retrace their steps. Once they arrive at their destination, most walking pilgrims on the *Camino* will simply take an airplane, bus, or train back home or wherever it is they are going next. They do not walk the route in reverse, although a few are now choosing this option.

As a variation on route versus destination, in certain instances pilgrims will instead spend much or all of their time walking in circles or circumambulating a sacred place or shrine rather than going directly to it. One famous example of a circumambulatory pilgrimage is in Tibet. Hindu, Buddhist, and Bon pilgrims will walk a more than thirty-mile circuit around Mount Kailash. Another well-known example is in India. Hindu pilgrims to Banaras will also often walk in a circular or spiral pattern around the city. Pilgrims are never allowed to ascend the slopes of Mount Kailash itself, while most pilgrims to Banaras will eventually enter into the heart of the sacred city and make their way to the banks of the Ganges.

A recent development in the United States is the growing popularity of walking a labyrinth as a spiritual exercise. While this activity is perhaps not the same as walking several hundred miles to a sacred place or shrine, it is at least reminiscent of the process. Labyrinths have a central destination, but the emphasis is surely on the meditative aspects of the circuitous walk itself.

Since ancient times, labyrinths have been found around the world. Walking labyrinths were constructed on the floors of European cathedrals when pilgrimages to the Holy Land were restricted after the Crusades, as a kind of substitute journey. Today, Americans walk labyrinths in a variety of settings from traditional churches to hospital grounds, college campuses, retreat centers, and public parks. Such a meditative walk or metaphorical pilgrimage has certainly struck a positive chord with a large segment of the general population, and perhaps it is like pilgrimage in being close to a universal image and practice.

> *What it may witness to is a deep-seated human intuition that present placedness only becomes fully worthwhile and intelligible if it is set in a larger context, and for that to happen a spiritual journey is necessary, with the journey itself an indispensable part of the learning process. The goal is thus not the sole aim; travelling is as much part of the pilgrimage and just as integral as the final objective.*[3]

It is clear that many different pathway configurations are possible. The exact details can be worked out over time and modified to local conditions and circumstances. A good strategy could involve thinking of ways that give pilgrims the greatest number of options. For example, pathways might be configured so that pilgrims can return to the same spot they departed from in the course of a day or even a few hours. Such a pathway might link into a broader network, so those pilgrims who want a longer walk—perhaps a trek lasting multiple days—could have that option as well.

SPIRIT

While there are other reasons why we might want to create new pilgrimage pathways in the United States, the central one is to provide pilgrims with an experience that speaks to their spiritual selves. American pilgrims are looking for occasions to nurture their soul. What are the best ways this could be accomplished?

Historically, pilgrims sought spiritual fulfillment at sacred destinations, whether that was a building, shrine, or some other feature imbued with the sacred or holy. Pilgrims thought they could best encounter their god or gods at the endpoint of their journey. Most destinations featured images and icons from specific religious traditions that clued pilgrims into the significance and meaning of the sacred place. Since a sacred endpoint will be less of an option in new American pathways, we need to think differently about how to make the pilgrimage experience richly spiritual without having a church, temple, mosque, shrine, tomb, or statue as the ultimate destination.

That can partly be answered by looking at what actually made such earlier destinations sacred or holy for so many people. Basically, the question is, what makes any sacred place sacred? The answer to that is not always straightforward and depends on a number of factors.

Many think that God, a god or goddess, or some other-than-human divine power is indeed what truly makes a place sacred. From this perspective the reason a place or shrine is sacred is either because the divine is actually present at the site or because the divine has created or designated the place in such a manner. For example in the Biblical Book of Exodus, it is written that God made himself present in a burning bush and as Moses approached, God cried out for Moses to remove his shoes as he was now standing on holy ground. Furthermore, any place so identified might have had no inherent sacred qualities before it is so designated. A grotto might have just been a common grotto until a divine entity such as the Virgin Mary made an appearance there. After the appearance or event, the place is never the same and is forever imbued with the sacred. Mircea Eliade might refer to this process as being a hierophany.[4] In short, it is the act or actual presence of the divine that makes a place sacred, holy, or spiritual.

One of the attractions of sacred space for believers is that they feel they can be near to and communicate better with their god or gods in such places. Two of the main functions of sacred space is that these are places where people can best communicate with the divine, and that such places are where divine power manifests itself in the form of healing and other ways.[5] While many Christians say that God is present everywhere, they feel that they have a better chance of being heard by praying in a church or at a shrine. Hindus talk about *darshan*—to see and be seen by the divine—which can often be achieved at pilgrimage destinations.

From this perspective, pilgrimage planners would need God, Mary, Shiva, or some other divine entity to make places or pilgrimage routes in the United States sacred by their presence or designation. This is beyond human control and difficult to imagine in the pluralistic country we have become. When thinking about creating new pilgrimage routes, it might be useful for planners to remember that they need not in and of themselves be sacred places in this sense of divine presence or designation. Rather, places along the way might be better seen more as gateways or windows to sacred realms. In Irish folk traditions, there is the notion that there are thin spots in the world—places where the divine and the human come into contact with each other. Such locales are not so much holy in and of themselves, but are instead apertures to spiritual realms. Pilgrimage planners might think more about what might evoke spiritual connection for pilgrims, rather than trying to convince walkers that a particular place is inherently sacred or imbued with the holy.

Most social scientists and secular scholars say that it is not God or some other divine entity but rather humans who imbue places with sacred qualities. In this view, there is nothing inherently divine, miraculous, or enchanted about locales or pilgrimage destinations that have been identified. Human beings, for various purposes and through various cultural and social dynamics, imbue certain places with symbolism and meaning that makes them sacred. In order to understand or analyze such places, you need to understand the symbolism involved, shared meanings, how people learn, and the power dynamics of a given society. Ellen Badone, for example, writes:

In the final analysis, it is necessary to recognize that the "sacred" is always socially constructed. Objects of cult, elements of the natural world, people and places become sacred through the meanings projected onto them by specific communities and individuals.[6]

How people project meanings onto place and how other people then learn to recognize and respond to a sacred space so constructed is not always clear, however. In what ways do people respond emotionally to something that has simply been designated as sacred by an individual or group of people? Are most people easily convinced that a god or divine presence is at a place, even though it was in fact some ancestor, priest, or powerful group's narrative or action that actually created the meaning or association? Implicit in this approach is that once you understand the source of the meaning and the power dynamics involved, you might no longer see the place as sacred and holy, or at least not in the same way. The goal of such analysis is something akin to the role of Toto in exposing the mortal behind the curtain who is projecting the image of the all-powerful Wizard of Oz. Such analyses might actually have the effect of reducing enchantment, the perception of the sacred, and spiritual connection.

On the other hand, such a perspective also holds out the possibility that sacred places can be created or at least reinforced by human actions. Pilgrimage pathways might be simply designed to evoke a sense of the sacred, knowing full well that this is a human act. Architects have been consciously creating sacred spaces for thousands of years. The gods or God did not design or build the cathedral, temple, or mosque, but many feel these places are indeed sacred and the divine might best be encountered in such structures. In many religious traditions, humans construct or designate a place and then have ceremonies or rituals that invite the divine to inhabit such locales and to sacralize them. Pilgrimage planners in the United States might also consider some kind of multifaith consecration once their pathway is constructed or designated.

Another way to think about what contributes to the construction or identification of sacred space is the idea that places themselves—apart from the meaning or modification given to them by people or cultures, or apart from any divine intervention—can contribute to making them sacred. Certain combinations of a place's topography, ecology, and other factors will necessarily strike a chord in the perceiver. Belden Lane refers to this as "giving voice to place."[7] Is there anyone who can look up to the stars on a clear night or stand at the edge of the Grand Canyon and not feel at least a glimmer of awe or a sense of the divine? Why is it that humans everywhere seem to be attracted to certain landscape features such as water bodies, caves, and overlooks?

Places and landscapes, apart from their social constructions and divine intervention, might be able to evoke spiritual feelings in humans. Rudolf Otto coined the term *numinous* to describe such a feeling.[8] In Otto's thinking, when a person encounters the divine, they are likely to have an experience with specific qualities or characteristics. One part of the numinous experience is what he called *creature-feeling*. This is the feeling a person gets when they encounter something so vast and powerful it makes them feel small and insignificant. The second aspect of the numinous is termed the *mysterium tremendum*. The *tremendum* part is the feeling that you are in the presence of glory, power, and the truly awesome. The *mysterium* is that we cannot hope to understand or express this phenomenon. It is not just unknown, but unknowable to the rational mind. The third aspect of the numinous is what he called fascination or *fascinens*. This reflects the fact that even though when we encounter the divine and it can be quite daunting and fearsome, we are nevertheless fascinated and drawn to it. It is as if our eyes are opened to true reality and once seen we do not want it to go away.

Otto said that the numinous might be triggered or evoked in certain ways. He also said there are ways, usually nonverbal, that the numinous can be expressed. Some of the ways the numinous can be triggered or expressed have landscape and place implications. Otto said that the perception of great distance, especially in the horizontal plane, can be one such way. He noted that certain landscapes created in East Asia were particularly good at this. He wrote that East Asian art, including landscape design, was adept at evoking such a feeling:

Empty distance, remote vacancy, is, as it were, the sublime in the horizontal. The wide stretching desert, the boundless uniformity of the steppe, have real sublimity, and even in us Westerners they set vibrating chords of the numinous along with the note of the sublime.[9]

Other writers have supported this idea. Antonio Gualtieri made the claim that the Himalayas would have a numinous effect on any person, no matter their culture or background. He noted numinous-like descriptions of the Himalayan experience by European climbers as well as Indigenous inhabitants of Tibet and other nearby areas. He found that the Western mountaineers wrote about their experiences in ways that seem close to Otto's perception. One explorer wrote:

These mountains of Asia, in their very vastness and remoteness, imprint themselves on the soul of the man who once sets foot on them, because they touch him at every human level: they bring him a mystic ecstasy at one moment, they remind him of his animal nature at the next. And through them he comes to know everything from nameless terror to the joys of scientific discovery.[10]

Other features such as water bodies, irregular rock formations, karst topography, and caves have been suggested as other ways that landscape or particular landscape features evoke the numinous. Caves are especially notable because they have so often been chosen or recognized as being sacred in a variety of religious traditions including Christianity, Buddhism, and Hinduism.

Many other writers, whether they were aware of the numinous or not, have noted that certain landscape characteristics often feature prominently in pilgrimage routes and destinations. Alan Morinis, for example, writes that "pilgrimage places so often ... are located in places of geographical splendor. Mountaintops, sea vistas, great rivers, and springs are easily translated into images of greatness."[11]

LIMINALITY

The notion of liminality was first developed by Arnold van Gennep in his book *Rites of Passage*.[12] He claimed that any liminal ritual first entails the individual's separation from everyday life and relationships. They then enter a liminal time period, where transformation takes place. It is during this liminal period when rules, roles, and everyday structures are abandoned. This gives the rituals a special quality and sacred power.

Although van Gennep and others writing on liminality focus on the temporal dimension of liminality, it is useful to note that liminality also can have a spatial component. Many sacred places around the world are perceived as being places that are betwixt and between. Thresholds, fords in streams, bridges, borders, divides, doorways, portals, and other physical features or spaces can and do serve as liminal places in a variety of circumstances and can help create or delineate sacred spaces. For example, Japanese Shinto shrine areas are marked off by *torii*, ceremonial gateways delineating the sacred area. Sometimes there can be as many as several hundred such gates put in close proximity in order to form a kind of entrance tunnel. Sacred places in India are called *tirthas*, but the literal translation is "a ford" or "crossing-over place." Many Christian churches have a series of passageways, doorways, and spaces a person has to traverse in order to enter the inner sanctuary and altar areas. Indeed, for centuries many Christians perceived the church itself to be a gateway to heaven, hence the need to be buried as close as possible to the entranceway. Christians also speak of "crossing over Jordan." Although the origin of the phrase refers to the Israelites crossing the Jordan River into the promised land of Canaan, it now has a number of metaphorical implications, especially now referring to the liminal space between Earth and heaven. Pre-Columbian Indigenous Americans in the Mississippi and Ohio Valleys selected sites for burial mounds that were in transitional places in the landscape, such as at breaks in topography, on the edges of bluffs, and in places where two streams converge or streams enter or leave a lake.[13] They seemingly wanted to bury their dead at major liminal places.

PILGRIMAGE VERSUS TOURISM

Some might say it seems like making pilgrimage pathways is no different than simply making regular hiking trails, and that pilgrims are not really different from other tourists. It is true that pilgrims have much in common with tourists, and pilgrimage pathways can in many ways resemble current hiking trails.

Pilgrimage, tourism, and hiking are all forms of mobility. Pilgrimage and tourism involve separating from one's everyday life and home and going on a journey, having significant and often intense experiences, and eventually returning home as somehow different and transformed individuals. Tourists bring home souvenirs, and pilgrims bring home objects and relics that help them remember their experiences. Often pilgrims become tourists along the way, and tourists can also become pilgrims out of choice or circumstance.

Writers now discuss such terms as "secular pilgrimage" and "spiritual tourism."[14] Most investigators see pilgrimage and tourism as at least interrelated or operating on a continuum. Certain pilgrimages might more approximate a touristic experience, while others have little in common with the typical tourist event. It could also vary by individuals even on the same pilgrimage or vacation trip. Many participants on the *Henro* see the experience largely in secular terms and as a leisure activity, such as walking to be in nature or to be with friends and family. Such an individual might be walking right behind an extremely devout pilgrim who is dressed in the traditional white costume and spends most of the time praying or conducting various ascetic practices at temples and along the route. However, that person who started out the walk in a secular frame of mind might have had unexpected things occur and subsequently experiences the latter part of the journey in a highly spiritual state. In such a case the question becomes not *who* is a pilgrim but *when* does a person on some kind of journey become a pilgrim?

Pilgrimage advocates and pathway planners in the United States need not worry too much about this question. If someone just wants to hike a pilgrimage route for fun or as a leisure opportunity, there would be little harm. They might be encouraged to avoid places on the way that seem to cater more to pilgrims. The only problem might be if their behavior, such as making loud noises, would somehow be disruptive to people trying to meditate or pray along the pathway.

Pilgrimage pathways would be different than traditional hiking trails in certain respects. Pilgrimage routes might purposely traverse a range of landscapes—including urban, rural, and natural. Most hiking trails are usually limited to natural settings and avoid features such as Superfund sites or low-income neighborhoods. Pilgrimage pathways might be organized in ways that provide services such as food, lodging, and rest stops along the way that more traditional hiking trails might avoid. Other features that relate more to spiritual experiences, such as places for the dead and numinous sites, might not normally be part of a traditional hiking trail.

Pilgrimage pathways perhaps share with tourism the fact that people might come from outside the local area and contribute to local economies, however. Pilgrims, like tourists, could spend money on food, lodging, and other local services. In this respect, popular pilgrimages can be seen as a significant strategy to diversify and enhance local economic conditions.

SENSE OF PLACE

Many writers, artists, and scholars have explored what it means to have a sense of place. This involves both knowledge of and emotional attachment to a particular locale. Having a strong sense of place is a significant factor in individual happiness and well-being. It leads to a stronger sense of environmental stewardship and also helps to develop or support strong communities.

Landscapes in the US are unfortunately becoming more and more placeless. There are few distinguishing features in increasingly standardized subdivisions and urban developments. Local materials and local architectural styles are rare. People do not live in places for long and consequently do not understand or care for them as much. Landscapes are less capable of evoking memories, meaning, and a sense of security and familiarity. Our everyday environments are increasingly corporate, monotonous, and superficial. Nonplaces might include the highway strip development and shopping malls, freeways, suburban tract developments, airports, and other such places. Few of us are aware of the *genius loci* of our local environments.

Greater participation in pilgrimage means that more people would be having more intimate and extended experiences with their local landscapes. Many would argue that this is exactly what we need—greater awareness and connection to our surroundings. Such enhanced awareness and connection might translate into better choices for new development and land use changes. It might promote better environmental stewardship, and would foster a stronger sense of community and shared ownership.

Principles for Creating Pilgrimage Pathways

There are six principles or criteria that could frame the conversation for anyone or any group thinking about coordinating, promoting, or creating new pilgrimage pathways. Below are summaries or elaborations of key principles touched upon earlier that might guide the development of new and enhanced pilgrimages for people in the United States.

THE EMPHASIS SHOULD BE ON WALKING AS WELL AS ON THE JOURNEY ITSELF

Putting more emphasis on the route and journey might mean putting less importance on any kind of ultimate destination. The emphasis on journey rather than destination and embodied ritual over creed seems to be the trend of how people prefer doing pilgrimage now as in the case of the *Camino de Santiago* in Spain, the *Henro* in Japan, Lutheran pilgrimages in Norway, and others such as the *Choʼŏndogyo* pilgrimage in South Korea.[1]

Creating new American sacred places is problematic in ways that creating new routes is not. Existing destinations in the US today include Catholic shrines, national monuments, selected wilderness areas, New Age power spots, and places associated with celebrities of one sort or another. These alone are not sufficient to meet the growing demand, either because they have limited constituencies or are in some cases inappropriate to our emerging values and sense of spirit. Rather than creating new destinations that all must somehow embrace, it seems more appropriate to focus on a route where a shared belief or religious affiliation is not necessary.

These shared routes should be made for walking rather than motorized vehicles. Walking pilgrimages have increasing appeal for people from a variety of religious beliefs and from a variety of cultural traditions. They also have the potential for creating far fewer environmental impacts than those dependent on motorized vehicles. A more meaningful pilgrimage experience coupled with a smaller environmental footprint make a strong case for not creating new pilgrimages dependent on airports, freeways, fossil fuels, and parking lots.

The spiritual and therapeutic advantages of walking pilgrimages are increasingly clear. Traversing a pilgrimage route on foot can be seen more as embodied and ritual mobility rather than simply a means to a sacred destination. Walking can help the pilgrim pray or focus on the experiential, meditative, and therapeutic aspects of the journey. Putting one foot in front of the other and experiencing the sights, sounds, and smells of landscape does not require any particular belief, membership in a denomination, social status, or ethnic identification. It is simply one of the most human things we can do.

Nan Shepherd spent many years walking the Cairngorm Mountains in Scotland. She wrote eloquently about her experiences and often emphasized the deeper knowing and spiritual awareness that comes from physical engagement and movement in that landscape. She claimed that walking for long hours evoked a "still center of being,"[2] and that the walking journey was itself part of the technique by which one's god is sought.

Tony Hiss coined the term "Deep Travel" to describe an attitude as one goes about one's journeys—one that includes developing a sense of awe and serendipity regarding the places and things encountered. He likens it to falling through the looking glass and seeing the extraordinary in the ordinary. Hiss's examples often center on walking experiences, such as the one he had

82

while traversing the High Line in New York City.[3] The High Line is built on an abandoned elevated rail line and is one of the most striking and unusual new pathways in the world today. It attests to the power and appeal of a walking experience even in the heart of Manhattan as it has attracted not only Hiss, but millions of visitors and pedestrians over the past few years. Similarly, Atlanta's beltline walkways and the linked pathways around the chain of lakes in Minneapolis give credence to the appeal of being able to walk significant distances through an urban area.

PILGRIMAGE ROUTES MUST BE USABLE BY PEOPLE OF DIFFERENT RELIGIOUS PERSPECTIVES AND AFFILIATIONS

Given the growing diversity of religion in the US and the rapid increase in people without any formal religious affiliation, it seems clear that new pilgrim pathways should not have features or elements that identify them exclusively with a particular religion or belief system. The pathways should be acceptable and useful to all—including those who consider themselves spiritual but not religious, or even agnostics and atheists. Americans already have an abundance of parallel land uses or structures in our landscapes. These include public roads, public trails, public parks, public mass transit, public schools, public plazas, and public buildings open to all. We should therefore have no inherent problem with creating public pilgrimage routes, open to all. This would not violate the principle of separation of church and state.

The First Amendment to the US Constitution guarantees the freedom of religion. This has generally been interpreted as stating that citizens should be able to practice any religion they choose—or no religion at all—without interference, coercion, or promotion from the government. However, one could argue that it is our human landscapes and infrastructure, not our government, that actually inhibit our ability to express or practice our religion if our religious practice includes pilgrimage. Walking pilgrimage is difficult or often impossible in the United States largely because of our automobile-based transportation systems and lack of public right-of-ways. This is akin to telling people, go ahead and practice your religion, but you just can't have a place to do so. This impediment to pilgrimage might in fact be closer to a violation of the First Amendment of the US Constitution even though it was largely unintentional. A person might be able to lead a spiritual or religious life without experiencing pilgrimage, but this limitation and de facto restriction is artificial and unfortunate.

Creating new pilgrimage routes should not be seen as a threat to individual liberty and the US Constitution, but rather as a public good and a way to actually increase our religious freedom. Governmental support, if necessary, could be justified on the basis that such routes can serve common human needs; generate economic, social, and environmental benefits; and would not privilege one belief or lack of belief over another. Newly created pilgrimages might even be better imagined as collaborative projects between various branches of government, along with religious bodies and congregations, local business and civic associations, environmental groups, health maintenance organizations, academics, professional planners, and any other constituencies or individuals.

A number of college and university campuses have already chosen to accommodate the religious needs and preferences of their increasingly diverse faculty and student bodies by creating singular spaces that serve as a spiritual commons for all groups. Some examples include the Pasquerilla Spiritual Center at Penn State, the Reflection Pool and the Meditation Garden at the University of the Pacific, and the Kay Spiritual Life Center at American University. Such facilities provide spaces to worship, pray, and gather. These common spaces do not have the imagery and icons usually found in places devoted to a single religious tradition. They could be used for interfaith services, or different groups can use the facility in a sequential fashion for their own purposes. These places can be beautiful and functional for all constituencies. They can promote interfaith understanding and dialogue. In the future, might colleges and universities likewise consider supporting common pilgrimage routes for use by their faculty, staff, and students?

Pilgrimage pathways, like designated buildings or spaces on campus, could serve as a framework or shell for multiple constituencies. Pilgrims would bring their own rituals and meaning to the route or perhaps an eventual destination. Imagine a mosque, a church, and a synagogue all located near each other. Then imagine a single pilgrimage path leading to these three destinations. Pilgrims of all three faiths could share the path, sorting themselves out at the end. Alternatively, there might not be any kind of an eventual destination, just a route that could be shared by all pilgrims. If pilgrims so desired, various activities, meditations, and rituals could be happily and satisfactorily performed along the way with no permanent physical alterations or ownership claims.

Although the route itself should have no permanent characteristics tying it to particular faiths, routes could nevertheless be customized by users with particular themes unique to one tradition or another. Christians, for example, might choose points along the way where different Stations of the Cross could be commemorated, much as they do at the Jasna Gorna Shrine in Czestochowa, Poland. Buddhists might similarly find places to remember the Four Noble Truths or the Eightfold Path. Individuals from any religious tradition could carry with them images, talismans, or other ritual objects and implements.

For pilgrims who still feel the need for a sacred destination uniquely associated with a particular religious tradition, privately produced and maintained side routes incorporating shrines or other types of religion-specific destinations could become optional linkages into shared routes. Pilgrims could opt to take such side trips to places not only associated with their own tradition, but with others as well. Indeed, the idea of a multifaith or interfaith pilgrimage discussed earlier would fit well with this model. Some routes could offer a variety of religious side trips for those so inclined.

Some existing facilities around the country might be repurposed to meet the needs of walking pilgrims. In many rural and even urban areas, Christian churches and other religious buildings are being closed or abandoned due to declining populations or declining memberships. It would be unfortunate to lose more of these historic and valued religious structures to the wrecking ball or forces of nature. Many such buildings could be put to use again as beautiful places for pilgrims to rest, receive meals, or stay overnight.

Another variation on this theme is that the few pilgrimage destinations we already have in the US typically do not have well-developed routes leading to them, especially walking routes. New walking routes could lead to old destinations. Many of the features discussed here could nevertheless be incorporated or adapted. Pilgrims might find, for example, that walking some distance to Mount Shasta or the Vietnam Veterans Memorial is at least as meaningful and transformative as their experience at the destination itself.

PATHWAYS SHOULD FOSTER SPIRITUAL EXPERIENCE

Although routes should not cater to one tradition or another, this does not mean that they have to be utilitarian, barren, or boring. They could be located, designed, and modified to facilitate experiences that would enhance and enrich pilgrimage from any tradition.

Routes could be planned with the maxim that they showcase or enhance the scenic qualities or beauty of the area. Aesthetic satisfaction is not limited to any particular faith, and planners could certainly use their expertise and work with local communities to create the most beautiful routes possible. The US Forest Service, the Bureau of Land Management, and various other governmental agencies in the United States already map and inventory the visual resources of the landscapes they administer. Such methods could be easily adapted to pilgrimage route planning.

Portions of the trail could feature gardens. Gardens play an important role in a number of religious traditions. Visualize verdant Islamic gardens that reflect images of paradise; Benedictine monastery gardens providing food, herbs, and medicine; the formal geometricity and symbolism of the Bahai gardens in Haifa, Israel; or the meditative Zen rock gardens of Japan. American gardens could at least provide a welcome rest and soulful respite for weary pilgrims along the route. There might be botanical gardens, flower gardens, or even arboretums. In areas where appropriate, native prairies, desert plants, forests, or other native ecosystems could be restored and showcased. Fruit orchards or food forests would be welcome additions and could actually help feed pilgrims. Memorial gardens could be both a botanical delight and a way to commemorate the dead. Outdoor labyrinths could be constructed as part of a garden complex or a garden sequence. While labyrinths are seen as a metaphor for pilgrimage, there is no reason not to have such "mini-pilgrimages" within a larger pilgrimage.

There could be places or stretches along the way that highlight works of art. Outdoor sculptures or sculpture parks could be strategically placed on pilgrimage pathways. Art can help pilgrims of any religious orientation think about beauty or express dimensions of the human experience that cannot be duplicated in any other way. A variety of sculptures adorn segments of the *Camino*. Beautiful architecture is a key component in most pilgrimages. Musical performances could be part of the pilgrim's experience.

Nondenominational structures could be built along pathways to enhance the spiritual experience of pilgrims. Altars, for example, could be used by a variety of different walkers. Places where pilgrims could leave or burn messages or prayers, or where candles could be lit, might be meaningful. On the *Camino*, there is a spot where people can leave behind a stone as a symbolic gesture of ridding themselves of some burden. So many stones have now been deposited that a substantial hill has appeared.

Liminality would be an enriching spiritual element to weave into pilgrimage pathways. Edges, divides, thresholds, fords, or other liminal spaces in the landscape could help focus the pilgrim's attention to the meeting of the material and nonmaterial worlds. Pilgrimage routes could be thought of as linear *tirthas*, places between worlds and realities—thin *seams* rather than thin *spots*.

Practically, this means that routes could include segments with sharp breaks in slope, such as the edge of a bluff or terrace. Routes could follow shorelines and riparian zones. Tunnels and bridges could be important symbolic as well as practical additions. It might be experientially significant or symbolically meaningful for routes to cross over watershed divides or ridgelines. In social and cultural terms, it could be meaningful for pilgrimage pathways to cross over political borders, territories, and neighborhood boundaries. Actual gateways and portals could be constructed, especially at the beginning or end of pilgrimage routes.

Pilgrimage pathways could be designed or routed in ways to trigger the numinous. Otto himself suggested that landscapes can evoke numinous experience. His wide travels allowed him to experience landscapes around the world, and these helped him develop ideas leading to his formulation of the numinous. He wrote that expansive vistas and open spaces are one way to promote "creature-feeling" and a sense of the sublime. Pilgrimage routes might therefore ascend peaks or tall structures or go along the edges of bluffs and escarpments that provide wide vistas.

Water features are often associated with the numinous. Pathways that lead pilgrims to the shores of lakes, ponds, streams, or wetlands of various sorts can evoke the *mysterium,* if not *tremendum.* Sacred springs can be found in the sacred landscapes of most religious traditions. Watery depths and the interplay of light and wind on water surfaces have fascinated and entranced people from time immemorial. Waterfalls are universally compelling and attractive.

Rock formations of the Canary Islands were an inspiration to Otto in formulating his notion of the numinous. Cliffs, rock formations, and rock outcrops do indeed seem to speak universally to human beings. It is apparent that the red rocks of Sedona have spiritual resonance to many in the United States. Caves and grottos figure prominently in most religions because of their chthonic mystery. Call to mind the Grotto of Massabielle at Lourdes (and thousands of its replicas) for Catholics, Amarnath Cave in India or Batu Caves in Malaysia for Hindus, Huong Tich cave at the Perfume Pagoda in Vietnam or the Mogao Cave Complex in China for Buddhists, ancient Mayan ritual cenotes in Mexico's Yucatan Peninsula, Hira in Saudi Arabia for Muslims, cave sanctuaries for the ancient Minoans, and hundreds if not thousands of other examples. If caves, rock formations or faces, cliffs, or grottos are in the vicinity then pathways might well take advantage of such opportunities along the way. Pilgrims would no doubt find them appropriate and numinous places for rituals, prayer, or meditation.

Another form of spiritual experience might simply be the feeling of bliss acquired through deep meditation or other kind of inward attention. This feeling is less the numinous encounter with a mysterious other and more about a feeling of unity and oneness. Pilgrimage routes could provide appropriate places for pilgrims to stop and meditate. Some would say that the act of walking a pilgrimage is in itself a way to meditate and evoke such a feeling of oneness.

Routes might strategically incorporate places for the dead, a key spiritual component of many pilgrimages throughout history. Pre's Rock in Oregon, the Imam Husayn Shrine at Karbala in Iraq, Banaras in India, and the *Henro* of Shikoku in Japan are just a few such examples in which a tomb or places of interment play a key role in the pilgrimage experience. Locations where the dead are memorialized or placed have enduring significance and can evoke the numinous. Funerary rituals, placing the dead in particular locations, and memorializing those who have passed on is considered a distinctive trait of humans, and archaeologists even use such evidence for its importance in defining *Homo sapiens sapiens*. Inherent in the word *pilgrimage* as it evolved in Christian Europe are the individual's own trials and tribulations before death and hopefully the eventual crossing over to the Promised Land.

New pilgrimage routes might do well to include stops or stretches where the dead are placed or can be memorialized. It is already one of the most common reasons for going on pilgrimage. Places for the dead can evoke thoughts of the pilgrim's own mortality and often sharpen their sense of who they are, why they are here, and where they are going. These places encourage musings on the great mystery and a focus on the meaning of life. Preexisting cemeteries or newly designed and constructed places for the dead, such as green cemeteries, could be incorporated along the way.

PILGRIMAGE ROUTES SHOULD BE LOCAL OR REGIONAL

For most people in the US today, embarking on pilgrimage means a significant amount of travel. This country has relatively few pilgrimage destinations, and depending on your own affiliation or preference, going to your destination of choice might entail a trip of hundreds or thousands of miles. For many it means going abroad. Such long-distance trips and destinations do not have to go away or disappear. However, they should not be the only or the most common option.

I would love to see the creation of hundreds, perhaps thousands, of local or regional pilgrimage pathways. These individual routes could be connected together to create larger networks. While some individuals might choose to walk a long distance via interconnected pathways, people should also be able to begin and end relatively close to home. Pilgrims should have the option to walk a few miles, hundreds of miles, or across the country.

There are several reasons for this focus on the near at hand. Local pilgrimage would reduce or eliminate travel costs, making such activities more egalitarian. Most pilgrimages today effectively exclude low-income Americans, as travel costs can be prohibitive for many individuals or families. Transportation, lodging, and meals on the road or at airports can translate into hundreds and thousands of dollars. Cost is not the only factor of course, and ardent pilgrims of any socioeconomic status might eventually find the means for conducting a pilgrimage. Nevertheless, it remains a substantial and unnecessary barrier for many.

A second reason supporting local pilgrimage routes is that they can help develop a sense of place and promote a sense of local stewardship and spiritual awareness. Few Americans have any depth of understanding and familiarity with the places they live. Most would be hard pressed to name more than a few species of local flora and fauna and probably quite unsure, for example, of the nature of the bedrock and other geological features. Their understanding of the historical evolution of the cultural landscape would likely be similarly fragmented or lacking. This lack of familiarity often leads to a lack of concern or ability to counter proposals and developments that would do landscapes harm. It certainly does little to promote a sense of the sacred near at hand.

A focus on local pilgrimage routes does not necessarily imply or promote a kind of shallow parochialism. *Deep* understanding and familiarity with a particular place and landscape does not negate a *broader* understanding. In fact, many would argue that it is a prerequisite. We cannot understand specific places or landscapes without being aware of what it takes to understand *any* place or landscape. A deep sense of place can be seen more as an aperture opening onto the world, rather than a perimeter.[4]

Ancient Romans believed in a *genius loci,* a spirit of place. They envisioned an actual spirit that reigned over each locality. The Shinto belief in *kami* is a similar example of other-than-human presence inhabiting a particular place. In traditional Japan, before beginning any construction or alteration of a place, the local *kami* needed to be recognized and placated. Modern Americans are less likely to imagine spirits inhabiting trees, waterfalls, or unusual rock formations. However, the Japanese created the *Pokémon Go* phone app, which places hundreds of other-than-human creatures in our everyday landscapes. The game caught the imagination of millions of Americans in a very short period of time. Could it be because, on some level, otherworldly creatures wandering our backyards and public spaces speak to our desire to see spirit in our local environments?

Geodiversity can also be important in creating a sense of place.[5] Unique landforms and outcroppings are also worthy of recognition and preservation. Local materials could give a local flavor to any buildings or construction projects. Imagine if people would simply use local stone or building materials instead of concrete or imported materials. How different our typical standardized constructions of today would be! A trip across the country or perhaps a long pilgrimage trek would give a dazzling array and a deeper understanding of the land being traversed.

Part of why Americans do not develop a strong sense of place is that they move often. Fewer Americans farm or work in the countryside. They seem to be spending less time outside of buildings or their vehicles. Americans as a whole don't walk much from place to place. Walking pilgrimages can counter this trend and put people in closer contact with the local landscapes where they live, and in so doing create an intimacy and attachment lacking today in many areas of the country.

Pilgrimage routes could certainly promote a better appreciation of the natural world, but they could also do much to develop an appreciation of the humanized and cultural landscapes of the United States. Experiencing landscapes firsthand is often a way to understand human history as well as nature. There are still landscapes that speak to American values and the story of our interaction with place and land. Pilgrimages bringing people into closer contact with such landscapes could foster the maintenance of rural communities and the preservation of historic buildings or neighborhoods in urban areas. They might inspire new forms of humanized landscapes that speak to our aesthetic, emotional, cultural, and spiritual selves. Much of the appeal of the *Camino,* for example, is the ability to experience the rich tapestry of rural and urban cultural landscapes and architecture of northern Spain.

Another benefit of local routes is that it is easier to have local control. One of the issues at many modern tourist and pilgrimage destinations is that there are often host–guest conflicts. In typical large-scale tourist developments, throngs of outsiders arrive. They might bring in desired revenue, but can also cause increases in crime, environmental degradation, infrastructure costs, and social conflicts or resentments. An attractive pilgrimage route might also bring in outsiders, but local landowners, governments, and civic organizations could better set the terms than, say, a large corporate resort complex. The dividing line between host and guest would be blurred as many or most pilgrims would be local themselves. Communal ownership of pilgrimage routes would promote and strengthen local communities. It would be one of the things about the place that people have a common interest in and could be a great source of local and civic pride.

Long-distance travel to reach pilgrimage destinations at the very least also means high energy consumption and high carbon footprints. One of the other main reasons for going local is to reduce the carbon footprint of pilgrimage in the United States. Air travel produces an especially high amount of carbon dioxide per passenger mile. Walking a local route mostly eliminates such travel-related impacts, and time spent walking is also not time spent consuming fossil fuel energy in other ways.

PILGRIMAGE ROUTES AND PRACTICE SHOULD PROMOTE COMMUNITARIAN AND SOCIAL JUSTICE GOALS WHENEVER POSSIBLE

The growing diversity of religious beliefs in the United States has already been discussed in detail. Apart from religious, language, and ethnic patterns, Americans are increasingly aware of other differences as well, such as gender identity and class differences. If new pilgrimage routes are going to cater to people from all religious backgrounds (or lack of religious affiliation), then as public spaces they must also be available and welcoming to people of all other kinds of diversity as well.

Pilgrimage advocates and activists might consider making the planning and implementation process inclusive from the very beginning. All voices should have the opportunity to be heard without privilege or discrimination dominating or interfering with the discussion. People of various religious backgrounds, along with African Americans, Latinx Americans, Asian Americans, and Indigenous Americans, could play a role. Pathway planning and production should be nonpartisan and should not be the province of any political party. Members of LGBTQ+ communities should have a voice. Residents of all socioeconomic classes should be represented. At the very least, the creation of new pilgrimage routes should not unfairly advantage or disadvantage any group.

Once completed, pilgrimage routes should be accessible to all. Those who want to participate in pilgrimage should not be stopped because of their income level, the color of their skin, their notion of the divine, or whom they love. This would also include people who are perhaps elderly and those unable to walk or walk well by themselves. For the most part, accessibility for all would be a matter of enforcing or strengthening antidiscrimination laws and policies already in place. For people who are unable to walk or have difficulty walking, there should be accommodations. Pathways, at least on selected routes, should be wheelchair and otherwise accessible.

Pilgrimage nevertheless can be a good way to promote community and communitarian ideals. Part of this would be to make sure there were places along the pilgrimage route where both large and small groups could gather. Despite the prevalence of social media, much of what we call community must take place in a physical location, or in this case on a pathway. Simple amphitheaters or seating areas of some sort could accommodate groups of pilgrims who want to gather for common prayer, meditation, song, or ritual, for example.

One of the prevalent theories of pilgrimage centers on the idea of *communitas*—a feeling of freedom from societal structures and roles and deep connection to fellow pilgrims achieved during pilgrimage.[6] The premise is that people on pilgrimage typically feel a deep bond with fellow pilgrims or even all of humanity.

Pilgrims throughout history and across the globe have spent a great deal of time interacting with fellow pilgrims, not only on the path, but also at places where they sleep and eat along the way. The English literature classic *The Canterbury Tales* is but one famous example that illustrates rich interactions at a pilgrims' inn. Many pilgrims over the centuries have written and talked about their experiences of spending time with other pilgrims at hostels, inns, restaurants, and other such places along the way. Pathways should have inviting places for people to interact with fellow pilgrims and share their experiences in a safe and appropriate setting. Figuring out how best to provide these services would be a challenge, but certainly local planning groups would be in an optimal position to create, or facilitate the creation of, such places that would suit their locale.

Some of the most popular American communal activities today are concerts and music festivals. Perhaps some pilgrimage routes could be tied into such venues or festivals. Imagine thousands of people walking to and from gatherings such as Bonnaroo in Tennessee or Burning Man in Nevada! Might not some of that same communitarian ethos be further fostered and extended by the walks associated with them?

Pilgrimage routes could also highlight social and environmental justice themes. Going on certain pilgrimages could make pilgrims viscerally aware of many of the social realities and injustice in our society. Most people know that in many ways our communities are still segregated by race, ethnicity, and class. Fewer have directly experienced what this means. Walking from high-income neighborhoods to low-income districts can be a revelation for people of any part of the socioeconomic spectrum or any religion. It would certainly give pilgrims many reasons to pray. Walking into parts of a city that are nearly all white or nearly all African American can have a similar effect on the pilgrim learning about race, class, and privilege. Done in a sensitive manner, such experiences could be transformative. I would hope that such segregation and huge income disparities in our cities will soon disappear as US society becomes more aware and just, but these seem an ugly reality for the present. Similarly, pilgrimage routes might help pilgrims better understand how pollution and certain types of development have typically had unfair and differential impacts on African Americans, Latinx Americans, or low-income communities.

ROUTES SHOULD PROMOTE ENVIRONMENTAL PRESERVATION AND RESTORATION

Pilgrimage pathways should be part of the solution to environmental problems in the world today, instead of contributing to them. Pope Francis has on several occasions, including his messages on the World Day of Prayer for the Care of Creation,[7] stated that polluting the earth or disproportionately consuming its resources is a sin. Along with many other religious leaders, he encourages people to acknowledge and even atone for the damage done to the earth and its ecosystems. There are at least three ways that developing new pilgrimage pathways could be part of the solution and atonement process rather than part of the problem.

The first is that environmental impacts could be minimized or eliminated to the greatest extent possible in the creation of new pathways and development of supportive infrastructure. This would mean, for example, that fossil fuel consumption would be greatly reduced. The focus on walking pilgrimages in a person's local area would be the main part of this effort. Beyond that, any buildings constructed should be as green as possible, using local and natural materials for construction. Heating and cooling could be done passively or with renewable energy sources. Water uses should be minimal and sewage treatment thoroughly complete before any wastewater is returned to the ground or surface water bodies. Toxic substances should be avoided whenever possible, or securely contained if necessary. Impervious surfaces such as paved parking lots and roads should be minimized and if large areas are created, runoff should be sent to retention ponds or otherwise treated before being allowed to enter nearby water bodies.

Such steps should be relatively easy to accomplish. Most routes would not necessarily need a great deal of new construction activity, at least nothing on the scale of, say, a new freeway. Walking pilgrimages should not require major new roadways and parking lots. Most areas along walking pathways would not need to be extensively landscaped or altered, or if so, native materials and appropriate techniques could be employed.

The second way new pilgrimage pathways could be more environmentally friendly is that they could help restore ecological health and cleaner water in each locality. Pilgrimage pathways could go beyond simply not causing damage to engaging in remediation or environmental restoration for neighboring activities and land uses. Buildings along the way used and financed by pilgrims could install solar panels beyond the capacity of what is needed for their own use. The excess electricity generated could be made available to local family farms or low-income neighborhoods. Pathway developers could construct stormwater retention ponds for nearby large impervious surfaces that they themselves did not create. Pathways could help promote vegetated buffer areas in riparian zones and along shorelines to reduce the impact from nearby land uses.

Pilgrimage pathways could both expand the area of wildlife habitat and create new corridors to connect existing habitat fragments. Ecosystem corridors connect patches of habitat and allow birds, animals, and even plants to expand their genetic pools and be more resilient in the face of various challenges such as climate change. Pilgrimage routes could build pathways for use by both people and animals that would go over or under transportation routes, such as freeways. Pilgrimage routes could thus simultaneously serve as pathways for humans and safe mobility zones for wildlife.

Green cemeteries would be one of the ways to preserve or expand existing habitat and natural ecosystems. Strict preservation of ecosystems and habitats that allow little or no human use will be increasingly difficult in the future. Human populations continue to expand and the number of places or acres that can reasonably be set aside in a pristine state in the US is quite limited. Instead, humans need to develop new and better ways to share the limited spaces on the planet with our fellow creatures. Green cemeteries are an effective and fairly easy way to accomplish this.

The third way new pilgrimages can help save the planet lies in using them to change pilgrim attitudes and behaviors. Simply going on pilgrimage can be a way to educate and inspire those doing the walking. The *Pad Yatra* pilgrimage is one such example. Several hundred pilgrims walked hundreds of miles through the Himalayas picking up trash as they went along. One purpose was simply to clean up some of these areas; but the pilgrims themselves learned a great deal about the environmental impacts of such debris, and about ways to alter practices and their own behavior in the region to reduce future waste.

Pilgrimages could have other environmental themes. Most Americans know the cities or counties they live in, but few are familiar with what bioregion they inhabit. Some pilgrimages might be designed to highlight such characteristics. Similarly, few people are aware of what watershed they occupy and what happens to runoff from their local communities or dwellings. Other pilgrimages might choose to focus on a theme of environmental disasters and perhaps restoration. A route that by went by the site of the Love Canal toxic dump or brownfields of one sort or another could make the human-caused damage quite apparent. Some routes might follow along coastlines that could be submerged in the future due to climate change, or skirt the devastated landscapes left by mountaintop coal mining operations.

Once pilgrimage routes are established, they could actually serve as deterrents to other, less environmentally-friendly land uses. For example, there might be more resistance to new mining operations or urban sprawl developments along cherished pilgrimage routes. People may be more open to mass transit or pedestrian-friendly transportation options instead of new freeways. Clear-cutting in forested areas might be less tolerated. Excessive development of shorelines and riverbanks might be avoided.

Many Christian theologians in the US today are reconfiguring their notion of the divine. In times past, the Abrahamic God was often seen as far away in heaven. He was seen as omnipotent and existing largely apart from earthly time and space. Pilgrimage destinations were often seen as portals or particular points where God could be contacted or His healing grace received. An alternative perspective and theology being developed is that God is here with us and in the world.[8] The pilgrimage pathway itself can serve as the gateway to the divine that is here with us and surrounding us.

Many people today, no matter their religious affiliation or lack of affiliation, simply see the environment and nature as part of what is sacred in the world. Treating nature itself as the sacred shrine or a focusing lens becomes one of the crucial components of pilgrimages in a new key:

We will recover our sense of wonder and our sense of the sacred only if we appreciate the universe beyond ourselves as a revelatory experience of that numinous presence whence all things came into being. Indeed, the universe is the primary sacred reality. We become sacred by our participation in this more sublime dimension of the world about us.[9]

1. Entrance/portal into the pilgrimage route
2. Statue garden
3. High point
4. Contemplative overlook
5. Reflecting pool
6. Cave or grotto
7. Waterfall
8. Ridgeline
9. Green cemetery
10. River crossing

7

Implementing
New Pilgrimage Pathways

For those who are now convinced of the compelling reasons to increase pilgrimage options in the United States and want to promote such initiatives, the question becomes, where to begin?

Any attempt to create a new pilgrimage route could begin with extensive discussions and multiple conversations. Articulating a vision and then bringing to fruition new pilgrimage pathways will likely involve numerous individuals, organizations, and various levels of government. It will necessarily be a communitarian endeavor from the start. Finding champions and allies, building bridges to connect people of various ideologies and faiths, conducting studies, and other efforts will be important. Engaged individuals might consider walking together as an appropriate first step.

How might a pilgrimage route be planned and administered? Where would the responsibility lie? Who would provide the funding? The answers to such questions will be complex, require working out over time, and will likely vary from place to place. If the focus is simply on property involved, then any route would at least be able to be mapped and described in legal terms. Some of the land might well be publicly owned or in public right-of-ways. Easements could be sought on selected properties. Individuals, institutions, or nonprofits could possibly retain the deeds to some of the properties involved.

Responsibility for the pilgrimage as a continuous pathway and activity is a more difficult question. Whoever owns a pilgrimage could determine the rules, pay the expenses, maintain the route, host associated activities and gatherings, and envision its design. Ownership of the pilgrimage would not necessarily belong to whoever owns the property, although these roles might intertwine with each other.

An admirable goal would be to give the entire local community a stake in owning the pilgrimage, much like communities feel ownership of the local sports teams, feel pride in a famous local landmark, or claim some famous individual from their area. New Yorkers don't individually own Central Park, the Statue of Liberty, or the Brooklyn Bridge, but most certainly identify with such features and have a vested interest in their continued existence and overall maintenance. Communities claiming ownership of pilgrimage routes in this way would be more willing to participate in their construction, appropriate use, upkeep, and growth. If people feel they have a voice and a vested interest, they are more likely to support improvements and resist changes detracting from the quality of the route. Many US localities have an Adopt-a-Highway program that could perhaps be adapted or expanded to become an Adopt-a-Pilgrimage program.

A good example of such community ownership of a pilgrimage can be seen in Japan. Several pilgrimage routes can be found on the Kii Peninsula and are generally referred to as *Kumano-Kodo*. The promotion and development of these traditional routes have taken new forms in recent years. Local community groups now commonly participate in conservation and trail maintenance projects. Other local people find employment and satisfaction in leading other pilgrims or providing therapeutic services. Nearby municipalities have experienced population growth due to people migrating to the area partly because of the pilgrimage attractions.[1] Clearly, the local community has become deeply invested in the successful use and growth of the pilgrimage.

INSTITUTIONAL STRUCTURE

Although ideally all community members would be invested, there should nevertheless be a smaller formal group in charge of day-to-day operations, administration, and planning. A legal entity should hold responsibility for promoting, developing, and ultimately maintaining a pilgrimage. The organization should be vested with authority and power by the participants and local communities to conduct business, purchase land, develop infrastructure, and make policies and regulations.

There are a variety of ways to legally structure organizations in the United States. The pilgrimage organization could be a government entity such as a commission or agency. An interfaith religious organization could perhaps take on the task. A flexible scenario would be to set up the group as a nondenominational, public nonprofit corporation such as the Nature Conservancy. As such, it could still partner with governmental, denominational, educational, and other groups without being restricted in certain ways.

A good example of such an organization is the Berkshire Natural Resources Council (BNRC) in Massachusetts, a nonprofit land conservancy organization. Over the past fifty years, they have acquired ownership or easements on more than thirty thousand acres of land and have worked with private landowners and government entities to preserve various tracts and develop hiking trails. Now the BNRC has started an initiative to create an interconnected network of land parcels and trails that they state is partly inspired by England's Coast to Coast Walk and the *Camino de Santiago*

Berkshires, Massachusetts

pilgrimage. They have named it the High Road and are working to create walking trails that connect natural areas, urban areas, and places of cultural interest. Hikers or pilgrims will be able to walk for days or weeks and have access to lodging, food, and other services throughout the system. The organization has a long list of donors, wide support in the community, and hundreds of volunteers who regularly help maintain the sites and trails.

TEAM FORMATION

Whatever institutional and legal structure is decided upon, individual members should be selected to fill positions of responsibility within that group. Organizing a group of enthusiastic, dedicated individuals who together envision a new pilgrimage route and then work to bring it to fruition might be the most important and significant step in the process. It would be a major accomplishment in itself.

The nature and composition of this group—similar to a board of directors—is critical for the project's success. Creating a new pilgrimage pathway demands a diversity of backgrounds. First and foremost, members should represent a range of religious backgrounds and perspectives—those from major religions as well as those who do not affiliate with any particular religion at all. Individuals serving should be especially eager to undertake an interfaith, or at least spiritually oriented, endeavor.

Board members should represent the large number of stakeholders needed for successfully creating a new pilgrimage route. Key government officials could be members of the group, serve as ex officio members, or at least participate in early conversations. Citizens representing civic or environmental organizations would be good candidates for membership. Professional planners could bring expertise, skills, and insights into the process. Health professionals and healthcare providers would be welcome additions. Individuals representing local economic development and business organizations could also have an important place at the table.

Criteria for membership could be further expanded. Organizers should take steps to include individuals representing various types of diversity in the locality. Ethnicity, race, class, age, gender, educational background, ability levels, and LGBTQ+ status are also important dimensions to keep in mind. The resulting organization should be representative and aware of the issues and concerns of these groups. If successful, this diversity could perhaps make such efforts unique among similar endeavors in the world today.

PATHWAY DEVELOPMENT

Once an organization and leadership team has been formed, the next central task would be to plan the pilgrimage pathway itself. Pilgrimage routes should be selected by a careful process involving all key stakeholders. What features the route encompasses and where exactly it would go would have much to do with the needs and desires of pilgrims and the physical characteristics of the existing landscape.

Although each region and potential pilgrimage route in the US will be unique, a series of questions common to all of them could be posed as the first step in determining the appropriate siting of a new pilgrimage route.

One of the first issues to resolve is to determine the length of the pilgrimage pathway. Most pilgrims should be able to walk about ten miles in a day, although that could vary considerably. Longer routes would need to include places where pilgrims could stay overnight. Since most pilgrims would probably not be campers, these overnight stops would need to provide food and lodging. Ultimately local pilgrimage pathways might be networked with others, allowing pilgrims to extend their journeys significantly if desired.

FACTORS IN PATHWAY ROUTING

A number of additional factors might then be considered when trying to determine the actual route of a pilgrimage pathway. These should be documented and mapped in order to make the best decisions possible. How to compile this information would depend on the expertise and capability of the planning group. Various maps would need to be consulted and produced. Many groups might choose to develop a geographic information system (GIS). Using a GIS can make gathering and analyzing extensive information easier and more modifiable over time.

Sample Pathway Configurations

DAY JOURNEY

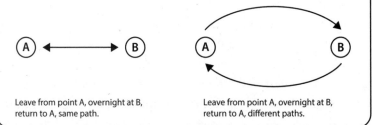

Leave and end the same place following the same path.

Leave and end the same place using circular paths.

ONE OVERNIGHT STAY

Leave from point A, overnight at B, return to A, same path.

Leave from point A, overnight at B, return to A, different paths.

TWO OVERNIGHT STAYS

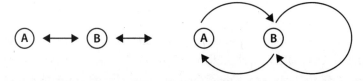

Leave from point A, overnight at point B, walk for one day on a single or circular path but return to point B for second overnight, return to point A.

MULTIPLE OVERNIGHTS — NODAL NETWORK

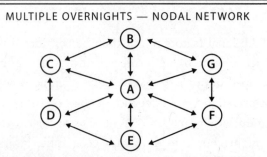

Leave from any point, choose from a variety of pathways and overnight destinations, one to multiple overnights.

No matter how the information is gathered, evaluated, and presented, the following is a list of features and landscape qualities that could help shape the decision-making process.

EXPERIENTIAL FACTORS

The primary purpose of pilgrimage is experiential. People go on pilgrimage for many reasons, as we know, but most are there for embodied experiences that speak to their spiritual selves. Although sometimes abstract, many aspects of the landscape related to spiritual experience can be inventoried and mapped.

i) Liminal Places and Features

There are features or elements in a landscape that can express the feeling of betwixt and between. Such features and spaces can be metaphors for the transformational experience that is pilgrimage. This list might include shorelines, riparian zones, ridgelines, watershed boundaries, sharp slope breaks, borders, boundaries, bridges, gateways, and tunnels.

ii) Numinous Landscape Features

Such features might include caves, exposed bedrock and cliffs, rock formations, surface waters (streams, rivers, waterfalls, rapids, lakes, ponds, wetlands, marshes, swamps, springs), and vista points.

iii) Religion and Culture

Religious structures, shrines, and sacred spaces would be key in this regard. Churches, temples, mosques, stupas, or shrines of various affiliations should be located before planning a route. Similarly, if there are natural features with recognized sacred qualities, such information should be taken into account. Pathway planners who want to give pilgrims a variety of side destinations could find this information especially significant.

Cemeteries should be located and inventoried. New pathways would do well to include existing landscapes for the dead. Many such places could allow pilgrims to linger or visit. Planners could also want to consider potential places for green cemeteries.

Historic sites, districts, and landmarks are also be important considerations for pilgrimage pathways. There might be significant historical sites that pilgrims would want to visit. This is especially true for pilgrimages that focus on social justice concerns, for example.

iv) Visual Resources

Areas of high aesthetic value could be identified. There are many valid ways to measure perceived scenic beauty. Careful studies can produce maps that show features and areas along with their aesthetic evaluation. Pilgrimage route planners could take advantage of this information in order to provide pilgrims with memorable aesthetic experiences.

ENVIRONMENTAL PROTECTION AND RESTORATION

Planners who want to protect and enhance the natural environment should carefully study the ecosystems and physical geography along potential pathways. Studies and mapping might include vegetation patterns or habitat types, surface waters, wetland delineation, critical habitats, the presence of threatened or endangered species, potential wildlife corridors, aquifer recharge areas, large impervious surfaces, possible sites for retention ponds, and steep slopes—especially those that might be subject to erosion.

SOCIAL FACTORS

It could also be useful to map income and poverty levels in the area being considered. Planners with special interest in social justice issues would surely want to know the locations of high- and low-income neighborhoods or districts. Route planners might want to include both or be especially mindful not to favor one group over another. Low-income as well as wealthy residents should have equal access. Routes that would potentially traverse certain neighborhoods should be done with residents' input and approval.

Patterns of population density and distribution might also be important. Many locals would use the route. Having nearby access would be a desirable factor. Places where pilgrims could access services such as lodging, food, and bathroom facilities would be key for successful pilgrimage experiences.

Planners should also note what political units (cities, villages, towns, counties, states) the route might traverse, and what kinds of regulations and permits each might require.

Ethnic patterns could also be significant. Depending on the goals, pilgrimage route planners might want to highlight certain ethnic neighborhoods or regions. An example of this would be Indigenous American reservations and ancestral homelands. Pilgrimage pathways should avoid Indigenous American lands, unless the residents and First Nations authorities invite such a use. In any case, pilgrimage planners should be aware of such areas in order to take them into respectful consideration.

LAND OWNERSHIP AND RIGHTS

Who owns what land, and what kinds of access might be possible, are critical considerations for pilgrimage planners.

Planners would probably find it useful to first identify public lands (federal, state, county, and local). It might then be easier to acquire rights for pathways through these areas rather than through private properties. Also, many public lands have features or qualities often attractive to pilgrims, such as forest preserves, wildlife areas, or heritage and historical sites.

Determining whether there are any public easements would also be important. Various public agencies have already purchased conservation or access easements that might be either used or useful in determining pilgrimage routes.

There are also private preserves and easements. A great deal of land in many locales has already been set aside for the preservation of wildlife or different types of ecosystems. The Nature Conservancy, for example, administers many such areas. With appropriate consultation and planning, some of these areas could be included in pilgrimage pathways.

The public already owns a number of right-of-ways, some of which might be used as part of a pilgrimage pathway. Planners would need to identify the existing network of roads. In some places, it could also be useful to identify publicly available navigable waters and access points.

HAZARDS AND BARRIERS

There are many hazards and barriers that could limit pilgrimage pathways, and planners should be aware of these from the start. These might include freeways, major highways, busy railroads, major airports, military bases, industrial complexes, landfills, toxic waste sites, and utilities and utility corridors (e.g., pipelines, major transmission lines).

PATHWAY ADDITIONS AND CONTINUING DEVELOPMENT

Once the pathway route has been determined and constructed, other elements could be added over time to improve the experience of pilgrims. Some of these would be basic service functions. Pathways could benefit from the addition of buildings for lodging and eating. Some buildings might be constructed primarily for restrooms, provision of drinking water, and showers. Other practical infrastructure might include emergency stations, signage, and gateways. Environmental restoration projects such as the construction of retention basins or alternative energy projects could be incorporated when appropriate. Any number of other additions might be added to enhance the pilgrim experience. Such initiatives might include art installations, labyrinths, gardens, gathering places, and ceremonial aids such as altars.

Most pathways probably could not be completed all at once. They might best emerge over time—especially if funding or other concerns limit immediate development. They could grow and evolve once pilgrims start actually using the route. In fact, a goal from the beginning might even be to evolve and adapt routes to changing conditions. Routes could provide richer experiences and accomplish new environmental and social goals over time.

Facing Challenges
and Moving Forward

Creating a network of pilgrimage routes in the United States implies change—to the culture, and more specifically to the religious or spiritual practices of Americans. It implies modifications of some magnitude to the landscapes Americans inhabit. The construction and use of new routes following the principles outlined here suggest changes that could be extensive and transformative but not necessarily easy or quick. Pilgrimage advocates and planners should be ready to make a long-term commitment. Many actions or attitude changes must simply unfold over the course of years.

Furthermore, creating new pilgrimages could be delayed or hindered by a number of barriers. Understanding and anticipating such roadblocks could help promoters and activists better prepare and develop strategies for dealing with them as they arise in the planning and implementation process.

ATTITUDINAL AND BEHAVIORAL CHALLENGES

Some of the barriers to creating new pilgrimage routes will be attitudinal and behavioral in nature. Will Americans widely embrace the practice of pilgrimage in any meaningful way? That remains to be seen, but there is already a great deal of momentum, so the prognosis seems good. More and more Americans are not only open to the possibility of participating in a pilgrimage but also are actively seeking opportunities to do so. They are becoming more aware of the value of pilgrimage and the possibilities it presents to enhance their lives. Since pilgrimage has long had almost universal appeal it stands to reason that most Americans would also be able to tap into this deeply ingrained impulse and find ways to make the experience attractive and fulfilling.

There is currently far less active opposition to pilgrimage than there might have been in historical times. Fewer Americans identify as Protestants, and most Protestants today do not share the same antipathy toward pilgrimage as some of the earlier leaders had. The problem now is less about countering active opposition to pilgrimage and more about dealing with a general lack of awareness or appreciation of the concept. Americans have never had a clear or widespread pilgrimage tradition and few people have ever completed such a journey. However, it seems that as more Americans learn about pilgrimages or have participated in walks such as the *Camino*, enthusiasm about the practice only grows. Advocates for creating new pilgrimages should therefore actively educate others about the possibilities and benefits. They might encourage those who have had positive pilgrimage experiences to share their stories and accounts.

The Catholic Church and the Mormon Church have long promoted pilgrimage in the United States for their members. Getting other religious organizations and denominations on board now seems like a real possibility and is in fact already happening. The benefits of increased pilgrimage activity for congregations are many, and leaders are becoming aware of the potential for enriching the spiritual lives of their members. Many leaders in Protestant denominations such as Methodists, Lutherans, Episcopalians, Baptists, and others already organize pilgrimages for their members. Positive treatment of pilgrimage appears frequently on their websites and printed publications.

The difficulty concerning denominational advocates may be that some such groups or individuals might be less interested in sharing pilgrimage routes with people of all beliefs or with spiritual but not religious folks. They might prefer routes with themes, iconography, and destinations unique to their own traditions. Interfaith initiatives and experiences may not be as much of a priority.

The challenge will be promoting the value of shared pilgrimage pathways for an increasingly diverse US population. Sharing a pathway does not seem to have caused problems on routes such as the *Camino*. Although it is a Christian-based route, it now attracts individuals from around the world and from a range of religious and secular traditions. Interfaith initiatives should in any case mutually support participants. Individuals worried about loss of faith or concerned about encountering challenges to their beliefs should be comforted and assured. Generosity and sharing are recognized virtues in all religions. Also, as discussed earlier, privately produced and maintained side routes and destinations specific to a particular religion or denomination are possible ways to fit the experience to the expectations and needs of people wanting such features.

Interfaith pilgrimage could be seen as a great opportunity to increase understanding. In the US today religious institutions are often the least diverse social groupings. People tend to worship and pray alongside those who look, think, and act very much like themselves. Although the details and ultimate destinations of a pilgrimage route can vary, sharing a pilgrimage experience with those that differ in belief and background might indeed help us create a truly pluralistic and inclusive society. The point is to not have everyone agree with one another, but to open a space where relationship and mutual respect are possible.

Promoters of new pilgrimage routes may face opposition not from members of particular religions or denominations, but from those who truly consider themselves atheists or have a strong anti-religion perspective. Some such individuals might say that the separation between church and state would be violated by any governmental involvement or support. They could insist that no public funds be used to create or facilitate pilgrimage routes even when such routes are not affiliated with any particular religion or denomination. They might not like any activity that seems to cater to spiritual or religious purposes, or scoff at those who want to engage in such activities, assuming they are operating under false pretenses and flawed thinking.

It wouldn't be necessary to completely change the minds of people oppos-
ing the creation of new pilgrimages on such grounds. One response to such
opposition is to point out that creating new pilgrimage pathways could have
real benefits apparent outside of the religious sphere, that are not necessarily
restricted to those going on pilgrimage. Even if not a single person ever used a
new pilgrimage pathway for pilgrimage purposes, creating such routes can at
the least promote a greener and more sustainable environment. The construction and maintenance of pathways and the provision of services to those participating in a pilgrimage could have social and economic benefits extending
to many in local communities. People do not have to go on a pilgrimage themselves or even like the fact that other people are going on pilgrimage to realize
that there are little harm and great societal and environmental benefits possible.
You do not have to use a public library to realize the value to a community such
an institution offers, and people who never plan on using a pilgrimage route
could similarly appreciate and support the creation of pilgrimage pathways.

Another source of resistance to the creation of new pilgrimage pathways could come from local and regional officials. Creating pilgrimage
pathways could have several negative implications for local governments.
Land or easements used to help create a pathway might qualify for tax-
exempt status and thus localities could stand to see a decline in tax revenue.
Providing police and emergency services to pilgrims could entail an extra
expense that would strain already limited budgets. Across the United States
local governments often struggle with existing commitments such as repairing
streets, updating water and sewer systems, maintaining parks, and adequately
paying for police and fire protection. Adding another financial commitment
might well be met with a skeptical eye.

Public safety on pilgrimage routes would certainly need to be addressed.
Pilgrims could be the victims of, or engage in, negative or criminal behavior
such as vandalism, arson, littering, theft, assault, and so on. If enough people
walk these pathways it would only be a matter of time before injuries or
medical emergencies would occur there. Pilgrims might end up getting lost
or stuck outside in dangerous conditions.

Public safety concerns alone should not be a reason to veto or dismiss
pilgrimage proposals. In the first place, it seems unlikely that pilgrims would

be a high-risk population as far as criminal activity is concerned. Furthermore, in the era of almost universal cell phone ownership and coverage most people could easily call for help. Safety stations could be included in the pathways and educational programs could help prevent some emergencies. As pilgrimage routes develop and evolve, more services could be provided along the way and reduce time needed for pilgrims to reach assistance.

One way to respond to financial concerns is to bring up the fact that there are both costs and benefits involved. What ultimately matters is the balance. Costs could be relatively low, especially compared with other infrastructure projects undertaken by local governments. Roadways, sewer networks, water projects, and park systems all come with much higher price tags. We know that pilgrimage routes could also provide a number of benefits to individuals, communities, and the earth itself. People could learn to live more meaningful, fulfilled lives. Community bonds and social capital could grow. Ecosystems could heal and flourish.

Pilgrimage routes might generate income or reduce costs in other areas as well. Popular pilgrimage routes could increase land values and actually increase tax revenues on adjoining or nearby properties. Property values near New York City's High Line have soared since its opening, for example. Businesses that cater to pilgrims might increase, generating bed and sales tax revenue. User fees could offset costs and liabilities incurred by local governments. Furthermore, new pilgrimage routes could also attract outside grants, endowments, and donations.

Ultimately it would be good to remind officials that pilgrims or others wanting to see the completion of pilgrimage pathways do also vote. If there is strong sentiment and support among the populace, then elected and other officials have a duty to carry out their wishes.

INFRASTRUCTURE BARRIERS AND CHALLENGES

The United States has well over four million miles of roadways. These are almost entirely designed, engineered, and devoted to the rapid movement of motorized vehicles. There are nearly fifty thousand miles of freeways alone. Freeways, or limited access highways, explicitly outlaw any other form of mobility other than motorized vehicles that can travel at high speeds. Pedestrians who do venture out to walk along open access highways, byways, and urban streets often put themselves at significant risk. Such routes, even if made safer for walkers, are rarely inviting and pleasant places to be. Simply finding a place to cross a highway safely can at times be a real challenge. Freeways prevent any crossings whatsoever along long stretches in both urban and rural districts and effectively create extended linear barriers for any cross movement of people.

It should be noted that the US has over 140,000 miles of railroad tracks as well. These, too, can be significant barriers to walking pilgrims or to the creation of new pilgrimage pathways. While some tracks have infrequent use by trains and would therefore be easier to negotiate crossings, many other tracks do have regular train traffic that could pose significant risk to pedestrians.

One of the greatest challenges to creating walking pilgrimage networks in the United States is dealing with a transportation infrastructure that has effectively blocked, marginalized, or banned pedestrians for much of the last century. Pilgrimage planners will be faced with the daunting task of either creating new right-of-ways that are devoted solely to pedestrians or figuring out how walking pilgrims and motorized vehicles can better coexist.

There is no immediate or universal solution to this problem. Most new pilgrimage routes will probably need to use existing right-of-ways for significant stretches, at least in the early stages of development. Many current hiking and biking paths have been able to take advantage of abandoned rail lines, and that might be an option in some situations. Hopefully pathways would evolve, and routes would better cater to pedestrians in the future.

Gasoline- and diesel-powered vehicles will diminish and ultimately come to an end. Oil will become increasingly scarce and expensive over the next decades. It is not a given that vehicles using renewable power sources will take their place entirely. Electric cars are still largely charged with electricity produced by coal and other conventional power sources. Will this mean the end or transformation of the vehicular network that currently extends across the continent? Will pilgrims be able to reclaim some of the roads in the same way hikers and bikers have been able to repurpose abandoned rail lines? Perhaps, but certainly not to any significant extent in the short term.

A transportation system centered on motorized vehicles has led to another major infrastructure problem: urban sprawl and exurban development. For the last seventy years urban population densities in the United States have regularly decreased as cities have expanded outward more than upward. In some US metro areas the urban densities are now actually lower than rural population densities in other parts of the world! Low-density urban areas have proven to be especially challenging to pedestrians. In such suburban zones there are typically few or no sidewalks. Many streets are dead ends or cul-de-sacs. Side streets feed into increasingly larger and busier roads, strip developments, and parking lots where much of the commercial and institutional activity takes place. Without access to a motorized vehicle, getting around millions of acres of sprawling suburbia is nearly impossible and almost always unpleasant.

A parallel development has been rampant exurban development. Millions of Americans now do not even live in a low-density suburb. They live far out in rural zones and commute many miles to go to work, to shop, or to play. Many technically rural areas have a greater proportion of residents not engaged in local rural activities than those who do farm or work in other primary local economic activities.

For pilgrimage planners, finding routes through such landscapes might prove challenging. In low-density suburbs there might be opportunities to use existing parks and parkways. In the countryside where increasing amounts of land are subdivided and devoted to housing, pathways will have to deal with fragmented ownership patterns and larger numbers of people who might be resistant to pedestrian traffic near their properties.

The overall rural settlement pattern in the United States is also quite different from the pattern in Europe and Asia. In Asia, Europe, and most other parts of the world rural residents traditionally tended to live in clustered villages surrounded by agricultural fields. In the US rural residents typically live on their own plot of land separated from other families. Especially in areas surveyed using the township and range survey system, individual residences could easily be a half or full mile away from the nearest neighbor. In Europe and Asia many long-distance pilgrimage routes can go from village to village, and pilgrims can find food and places to rest. In the US this is usually not an option. The net effect of low-density and dispersed rural settlement is that walking pilgrims in such areas would find it challenging to locate places to eat and sleep, or provide other services along their journey.

PROPERTY, PROPERTY RIGHTS, AND LANDSCAPE COMMODIFICATION

America has a long tradition of transforming the natural environment into a commodity or "real estate" by government survey and decree. Colonial and early American governments systematically transferred newly defined property to private owners. Many of the earliest immigrants to the United States were coming from a country going through a wrenching process of privatization of land rights. British Enclosure Acts in the eighteenth and nineteenth centuries took communal estates and carved them up into parcels of privatized property. Poorer members of society did not fare well and were ousted from their traditional villages and lands in the process. The colonies offered some of these displaced farmers a prospect to acquire deeds to their own property and set up their own "estates."

Much of American history is the story of taking land from the First Peoples, drawing up lines that carved the landscapes into vast checkerboards or jigsaw puzzles, and then allocating these newly created parcels to a select group of individuals who by some combination of hard work, circumstance, and privilege were able to acquire the rights. The US government simply *gave* away rights to millions of acres of land in the 1800s to railroads and other private companies.

Every society creates a land tenure system—a set of rules and practices that defines and then allocates rights to land and resources. It is necessary, and indeed one of government's main functions, to devise and monitor whatever system they create for the general welfare of the populace. Property and property rights are not created or distributed by God or somehow inherent in human nature. They are socially constructed and vary from society to society and from period to period. Such rules and practices should be evaluated and perhaps modified regularly to ensure that the system is doing what it is intended to do and best serves the common good. People may disagree about how to allocate rights and what constitutes the general welfare, but they cannot say that governments do not have the ability and the duty to create and then revise the system on a regular basis.

Governments in the United States have historically opted to give owners a generous package of rights associated with a property deed. Such rights typically include the right to use the land for their chosen purpose and the right of exclusive use. However, governments have always retained the right of eminent domain—the right to reclaim ownership of a piece of property if needed for a public purpose such as a school or road. Governments have also generally chosen to exercise their ability to extract payments from those holding ownership rights in the form of property taxes.

In other ways, US property rights have often been modified and changed over time. Governments at various levels have strengthened their ability to dictate what kinds of land uses are allowable, such as in zoning ordinances. Some ethicists and legal scholars are now considering possibilities such as giving plants and animals rights. Property owners in the future might have to take the rights of the whole ecosystem into account when making decisions affecting their portion of the earth's surface.

What has not been as well developed in the United States as in other countries like the United Kingdom or the Scandinavian countries are rights associated with pedestrians and access easements. There was a long history dating back to medieval times in the United Kingdom of common pathways. Such rights were often revoked or greatly diminished during the enclosure period. For many years, common people struggled to recreate or reinstate such rights. They have often been successful. In modern times pedestrian right-of-ways have increasingly been enshrined in law and most large property owners must allow people to walk across their land. In Scotland, the "right to roam" is even more explicit in giving people the right to walk freely across most of the countryside. It might be easier now to walk across the length of Britain than it is to go even short distances in the US where "no trespassing" rules hinder such movement to a much greater extent.

Since governments in the US never formally established strong pedestrian rights to begin with, Americans face a greater challenge. To institute strong right-of-ways or a "right to roam" would be a significant departure from historical land rights and land law. Currently, if planners and advocates want to create a pilgrimage pathway through or across private property, they would need to convince the property owner to legally transfer that particular right. The landowner could voluntarily sell them that right by outright fee simple purchase or by an easement. The landowner could also donate the land or an access easement. In any case, the party holding the deed has to be a willing participant.

Eminent domain could in theory be used. It is commonly employed in a number of other situations. In the US, government entities may even transfer the power of eminent domain to a private corporation, to force landowners to sell their property to the company in order to complete pipeline or powerline projects. Some city governments have used the power of eminent domain to facilitate urban renewal or economic development projects. It has long been used to create new roads, schools, and defense projects. Therefore, there is no inherent reason eminent domain could not be used to create pilgrimage routes. However, it would likely be contested by some landowners, and prove politically perilous in today's contentious climate.

Pilgrimage planners must then in the short term work within existing land rights and ownership patterns. Purchasing right-of-ways could prove to be expensive or even impossible if landowners are unwilling to cooperate. This is probably the second most significant barrier and challenge to the implementation of pilgrimage routes.

However, as in so many other ways, American attitudes and practice are evolving. Landowners in many areas might welcome the prospect of selling at least an easement or donating land as part of their legacy, or simply for tax or financial reasons. Liability concerns can be addressed in a number of ways. In many parts of the country there is already a significant amount of public lands. The US is a large country containing millions of acres lying idle or seldom used. As Woody Guthrie reminded us in his American anthem, "This Land Is Your Land," there is also a strong folk sentiment and moral argument for greater access to the countryside. Americans have never been entirely comfortable with their increasing exclusion from the landscapes they live in. Citizens can make change happen if they see the public value and inherent worth. Many people did not like the idea of zoning when it was first introduced, but zoning is widely accepted now as a useful tool in promoting the common good. The public may increasingly believe that a pilgrimage pathway is indeed a higher purpose land use. Pilgrimage planners and local landowners could pursue a mix of approaches resulting in responsible access and the ability to create pathways acceptable to all involved.

MOVING FORWARD

Creating new pilgrimage routes has the potential to be challenging and difficult. So why bother? If someone really wants to have a pilgrimage experience, let them go off to Europe or Asia, where opportunities more readily present themselves. We have enough other problems to deal with that seem to demand our more immediate attention. Is creating new pilgrimage routes truly worth the time, money, and effort involved?

Hopefully the answer for many will be yes. This book has discussed numerous reasons why creating new pilgrimages in the United States on a local and regional basis would be a positive, valuable endeavor. For individuals, pilgrimages hold out the promise of experiencing richer spiritual lives, healing, forgiveness and atonement, health and wellness, the ability to mourn, and finding better ways of dealing with difficult transitions in our lives. Pilgrimages can encourage community bonds, help people to better embrace and deal with our growing diversity, and promote social and environmental justice. Of increasing importance in the twenty-first century, new pilgrimage routes and traditions can do much to promote a greener and more sustainable world.

Many of the biggest problems we face in the world today do not lend themselves well to easy solutions. Solving the climate crisis, for example, entails dealing with multiple perspectives and multiple constituencies. Any actions taken will undoubtedly involve numerous trade-offs and affect individuals and communities in different ways. Climate change will never be solved in the way a math equation might be solved, but there are certainly better and worse approaches. Doing nothing or opting for business as usual is probably the worst choice.

No one really knows all the dimensions of the climate change problem, and certainly solutions will have to be complex and far ranging. Creating new pilgrimage routes will not in itself solve the problem, but it could help. Similarly, new pilgrimages across the country will not stop the rapid decline in biodiversity, but they might play a key role in saving some species from extinction and increasing the prevalence and populations of others. Pilgrimage will not solve all of our social and personal problems, but it could begin the process of healing and building stronger communities. New pilgrimages and pilgrimage routes will not save the world, but they could help repair it.

What the creation of new pilgrimage routes can do at the very least is simply give ordinary people the opportunity to do something. The scale of personal and societal problems we all face can overwhelm individuals. It is easy to tell ourselves that there is nothing we can do or what little we can do won't make a difference. Creating new pilgrimage routes and participating in pilgrimage walks can give people the personal and collective means to change the narrative. It can foster hope rather than despair. A single individual or even a local community cannot stop the loss of the polar ice cap or rid the country of prejudice and discrimination. Individuals and local communities can take some action, however, and what they do accomplish can make a real difference.

AMERICAN EXCEPTIONALISM REVISITED

For much of the last 250 years the United States has been exceptional by global standards and historical measures, in that we have not created many pilgrimage routes or regularly participated in such walks. Perhaps the time has come to create a country that is not only more in sync with the rest of humanity, but also goes beyond and even inspires the creation of new pilgrimages around the world. We can learn from but not necessarily copy pilgrimages such as the *Camino,* the *Henro,* or the *Hajj.* The United States has a different history and we should make pilgrimages in this country fit who we are now as a people and what kinds of landscapes we want to live in.

The United States of America has long been a beacon of hope for people around the world. It has been a country that ideally exemplified and promoted democratic principles, strived for justice, embraced people of various backgrounds, celebrated natural wonders, carefully stewarded the landscapes of North America, and had a population that was truly religious and spiritually inclined. I would like to believe that this is still true. In this sense, creating new pilgrimage routes could be seen as deeply embedded in the American psyche and a sincerely patriotic act. It can be a way to celebrate the best of what it means to be an American.

Unfortunately, it is also true that the United States and Americans have not always lived up to such ideals. As often as we have promoted justice for all we have failed African Americans, Indigenous Americans, and many others. As often as Lady Liberty has welcomed the tired, poor, and huddled masses, we have excluded others or made them unwelcome. As often as we have preserved a free-flowing stream or mountain wilderness we have polluted other waterways and wreaked havoc on agricultural and forested lands. As often as we have followed our religious commandments to love our neighbor and share with the poor, we have also promoted hate and allowed massive wealth to concentrate in the hands of the few. While we espouse freedom of religion, we have not always been happy with the results.

Creating new pilgrimage pathways can thus be a way to collectively atone for our failures and lapses. Atonement has traditionally been the act of an individual as a response to a sin or failure on their part. Pilgrimages can still provide that opportunity for individuals, but new pilgrimage routes can also accomplish atonement on a societal level. If it is a sin to destroy the environment, then perhaps creating a green pilgrimage pathway would be one way to make amends in that direction. We cannot undo the sins of religious and racial intolerance, but we can integrate service, better understanding, and healing into the pilgrimage experience.

Creating new pilgrimages is a powerful way to demonstrate what our true priorities are. If the main goal of life in America is for individuals to get rich in any way possible, then there is little hope. We have too often been willing to sacrifice the environment and the well-being of others to accomplish this feat. If our goals focus more on spiritual growth, the flourishing of community, and the health of the interrelated web of life, then pilgrimage is a way to affirm and assert these priorities to ourselves and the world.

Creating new pilgrimage pathways is eminently possible. It does not require new technologies or scientific breakthroughs. It would not entail the kinds of costs other infrastructure projects require. Creating new pilgrimages is already within the realm of possibility for almost every community or group of dedicated individuals in the country.

Can we now begin?

NOTES

Chapter 2: Pilgrimage

1 Linda Kay Davidson and David M. Gitlitz, *Pilgrimage: From the Ganges to Graceland* (Santa Barbara: ABC-CLIO, 2002).

2 Alan Morinis, ed., *Sacred Journeys: The Anthropology of Pilgrimage*, Contributions to the Study of Anthropology 7 (Santa Barbara: Greenwood Press, 1992), 4.

3 Justine Digance, "Religious and Secular Pilgrimage: Journeys Redolent With Meaning," in *Tourism, Religion and Spiritual Journeys*, ed. Dallen J. Timothy and Daniel H. Olsen (Abingdon-on-Thames, UK: Routledge, 2006), 38.

4 Robert Macfarlane, "Rites of Way: Behind the Pilgrimage Revival," *The Guardian*, June 15, 2012, www.theguardian.com.

5 Michael A. DiGiovine, "Pilgrimage: Communitas and Contestation, Unity and Difference—An Introduction," *Tourism Review* 59, no. 3 (2011): 249.

6 Carolyn V. Prorok, "Transplanting Pilgrimage Traditions in the Americas," *Geographical Review* 93, no. 3 (2003): 284.

7 "News Archive, January 31, 2012: ARC Discusses Pilgrimage on the BBC's Beyond Belief Programme," Alliance of Religions and Conservation, accessed July 12, 2020. www.arcworld.org/news.asp?pageID=517.

8 Daniel Hitchens, "Pilgrimage's Progress: One of Britain's Oldest Christian Traditions is Reviving in a Strange New Form, *The Spectator*, July 16, 2016, 22.

9 Nieves Herrero, "Reaching Land's End: New Social Practices in the Pilgrimage to Santiago de Compostela," *International Journal of Iberian Studies* 21, no. 2 (2008): 131–148.

10 Sandra Scham, "The World's First Temple," *Archaeology* November/December 2008, 22–27.

11 Roff Smith, "Before Stonehenge," *National Geographic*, August 2014, 26–51.

12 Diana Eck, *India: A Sacred Geography* (New York: Harmony Books, 2012).

13 Bulbul Siddiqi, "'Purification of Self': *Ijtema* as a New Islamic Pilgrimage," *European Journal of Economic and Political Studies* 3 (2010): 133–150.

14 Peter Eeckhout, "Change and Permanency on the Coast of Ancient Peru: The Religious Site of Pachacamac," *World Archaeology* 45, no. 1 (1994): 137–160; Helene Silverman, "The Archaeological Identification of an Ancient Peruvian Pilgrimage Center," *World Archaeology* 26, no. 1 (1994): 1–18.

15 Guillermo Salas Carreno, "The Glacier, the Rock, the Image: Emotional Experience and Semiotic Diversity at the Quyllurit'i Pilgrimage, Cuzco, Peru," *Signs and Society* 2, no. S1 (2014); Michael J. Sallnow, *Pilgrims of the Andes: Regional Cults in Cusco* (Washington, DC: Smithsonian Institution Press, 1987).

16 Seyyed Hossein Nasr, "Pilgrimage: The Heart of Islam" (lecture, Washington National Cathedral, Washington, DC, December 2, 2003).

17 Ian Reader, *Making Pilgrimages: Meaning and Practice in Shikoku* (Honolulu: University of Hawai'i Press, 2006).

18 Jean Dalby Clift and Wallace B. Clift, *The Archetype of Pilgrimage: Outer Action with Inner Meaning* (Mahwah, NJ: Paulist Press, 1996).

19 Phil Cousineau, *The Art of Pilgrimage: The Seeker's Guide to Making Travel Sacred,* anniversary ed. (San Francisco: Conari Press, 2012).

20 Rosemary Mahoney, *The Singular Pilgrim: Travels on Sacred Ground* (New York: Houghton Mifflin Harcourt, 2003).

21 *The Way,* DVD, directed by Emilio Estevez (Barcelona: Filmax; Elixir Films, 2010).

22 Rachel Joyce, *The Unlikely Pilgrimage of Harold Fry: A Novel* (New York: Random House, 2013).

Chapter 3: Pilgrimage in the United States

1 Wilber Zelinsky, "The Uniqueness of the American Religious Landscape," *Geographical Review* 91, no. 3 (2001): 569.

2 "In Depth: Religion," Gallup, accessed July 12, 2020. https://news.gallup.com/poll/1690/religion.aspx.

3 Martin Luther, *To the Christian Nobility of the German Nation,* annotated study guide ed. (1520; repr., Minneapolis: Fortress Press, 2016).

4 Juan Eduardo Campo, "American Pilgrimage Landscapes," *Annals of the American Academy of Political and Social Science* 558 (1998): 44.

5 Carolyn V. Prorok, "Transplanting Pilgrimage Traditions in the Americas," *Geographical Review* 93, no. 3 (2003): 283–307.

6 For example, see Linda Graber's *Wilderness as Sacred Space* (Association of American Geographers, 1976) or Edward Abbey's *Desert Solitaire: A Season in the Wilderness* (New York: Touchstone Books. 1990).

7 Campo, "American Pilgrimage Landscapes," 48.

8 Rebecca Solnit, *Wanderlust: A History of Walking* (New York: Viking-Penguin, 2000): 60.

9 *Sacred Journeys with Bruce Feiler,* DVD, directed by Leo Eaton (Boston: WGBH Educational Foundation: Maya Vision International, 2014).

10 "America's Changing Religious Landscape," Pew Research Center, accessed July 12, 2020. www.pewforum.org/2015/05/12/americas-changing-religious-landscape.

11 "In U.S., Decline of Christianity Continues at a Rapid Pace," Pew Research Center, accessed July 12, 2020. www.pewforum.org/2019/10/17/in-u-s-decline-of-christianity-continues-at-rapid-pace.

12 Adrian Ivakhiv, "Power Trips: Making Sacred Space through New Age Pilgrimage," in *Handbook of New Age*, ed. Daren Kemp and James R. Lewis (Leiden: Brill Publishing, 2007): 263–286.

13 Curtis Coats, "Is the Womb Barren? A Located Study of Spiritual Tourism in Sedona, Arizona, and Its Possible Effect on Eco-consciousness," *Journal for the Study of Religion, Nature and Culture* 2, no. 4 (2008): 483–507.

14 Coats, "Is the Womb Barren?" 498.

15 Lynn Huntsinger and Maria Fernandez-Gimenez, "Spiritual Pilgrims at Mount Shasta, California," *Geographical Review* 90, no. 4 (2000): 536.

16 Robert J. Kruse, II, "Imagining Strawberry Fields as a Place of Pilgrimage," *Area* 35, no. 2 (2003): 154–162.

17 Jill Dubisch, "Healing 'the Wounds That Are Not Visible': A Vietnam Veterans' Motorcycle Pilgrimage," in *Pilgrimage and Healing*, ed. Jill Dubisch and Michael Winkelman (Tucson: University of Arizona Press (2005): 135–154.

18 "Run for the Wall: We Ride for Those Who Can't," Run for the Wall, accessed July 12, 2020. https://rftw.us.

19 Tyra Olstad, *Zen of the Plains: Experiencing Wild Western Places*, Southwestern Nature Writing Series (Denton: University of North Texas Press, 2014).

20 Sophie Haigney, "How Stone Stacking Wreaks Havoc on National Parks," *New Yorker*, December 2, 2018.

21 Mike Grimshaw, "Sheilas on the Move? Religion, Spirituality, and Tourism," *Journal of Religious History* 37, no. 4 (2013): 541–552.

Chapter 4: Pilgrimage's Untapped Potential in the United States

1 Loren Eiseley, *The Immense Journey* (New York: Vintage Books, 1959): 125.

2 Surinder M. Bhardwaj, "Single Religion Shrines, Multireligion Pilgrimages," *The National Geographical Journal of India* 33, no. 4 (1987): 457–468.

3 Allison Williams, "Spiritual Therapeutic Landscapes and Healing: A Case Study of St. Anne de Beaupre, Quebec, Canada," *Social Science and Medicine* 70 (2010): 1633–1640.

4 Wil Gesler, "Lourdes: Healing in a Place of Pilgrimage," *Health and Place* 2, no. 2 (1996): 95–105.

5 Jill Dubisch and Michael Winkelman, eds., *Pilgrimage and Healing* (Tucson: University of Arizona Press, 2005), xxxvi.

6 Catrien Notermans, "Loss and Healing: A Marian Pilgrimage in Secular Dutch Society," *Ethnology* 46, no. 3 (2007): 1–17.

7 Kumi Kato and Ricardo Nicolas Progano, "Spiritual (Walking) Tourism as a Foundation for Sustainable Destination Development: Kumano-ko Pilgrimage, Wakayama, Japan," *Tourism Management Perspectives* 24 (2017): 243–251.

8 William S. Schmidt, "Transformative Pilgrimage," *Journal of Spirituality in Mental Health* 11 (2009): 66–77.

9   *The Way*, DVD, directed by Emilio Estevez (Barcelona: Filmax; Elixir Films. 2010).

10 Rachel Joyce, *The Unlikely Pilgrimage of Harold Fry: A Novel* (New York: Random House, 2013).

11 Diana Eck, *Banaras: City of Light* (New York: Columbia University Press, 1998).

12 Robert Putnam, "Bowling Alone: America's Declining Social Capital," *Journal of Democracy* 6, no. 1 (1995): 65–78.

13 Andres Duany, Elizabeth Plater-Zyberk, and Jeff Speck, *Suburban Nation: The Rise of Sprawl and the Decline of the American Dream* (New York: North Point Press, 2000).

14 Larry L. Rasmussen, *Earth-Honoring Faith: Religious Ethics in a New Key* (Oxford: Oxford University Press, 2013).

15 Sally Welch, *Pilgrimage*, YouTube video, 57:12, Accessed July 12, 2020, www.youtube.com/watch?v=8OiFcneW3tw.

16 Jason Danely, "A Watchful Presence: Aesthetics of Well-Being in a Japanese Pilgrimage," *Ethnos* 82, no.1 (2017): 165–192.

17 Justine Digance, "Religious and Secular Pilgrimage: Journeys Redolent With Meaning," in *Tourism, Religion and Spiritual Journeys*, ed. Dallen J. Timothy and Daniel H. Olsen (Abingdon-on-Thames, UK: Routledge, 2006): 36.

18 Francis, *Laudato Si' (On Care for Our Common Home)* (Vatican City: Vatican Press, 2015).

19 "Green Pilgrimage Network," Alliance of Religions and Conservation, accessed July 12, 2020. www.arcworld.org/projects.asp?projectID=521.

20 *Pad Yatra: A Green Odyssey*, DVD, directed by Wendy J. N. Lee (Los Angeles: Good Docs Films, 2013).

21 Michael L. Rosenzweig, *Win-Win Ecology: How the Earth's Species Can Survive in the Midst of Human Enterprise* (Oxford: Oxford University Press, 2003).

22 "Introducing the A2A Trail—A Pilgrimage for Nature," Algonquin to Adirondacks Collaborative, accessed July 12, 2020. www.a2acollaborative.org.

23 Mary Esch, "Wandering Moose Inspires 400-Mile Cross-Border Trail," Associated Press, August 13, 2016.

24 Jonathon Z. Smith, *To Take Place: Toward Theory in Ritual* (Chicago: University of Chicago Press, 1987).

25 Douglas Burton-Christie, "The Gift of Tears: Loss, Mourning and the Work of Ecological Restoration," *Worldviews* 15 (2011): 37.

Chapter 5: Pathway, Spirit, and Place

1   Anna Davidsson Bremborg, "Creating Sacred Space by Walking in Silence: Pilgrimage in a Late Modern Lutheran Context," *Social Compass* 60, no. 4 (2013): 557.

2   Michael J. Sallnow, *Pilgrims of the Andes: Regional Cults in Cusco* (Washington, DC: Smithsonian Institution Press, 1987).

3 David Brown, *God and Enchantment of Place: Reclaiming Human Experience* (Oxford: Oxford University Press, 2006): 232.

4 Mircea Eliade, *The Sacred and the Profane: The Nature of Religion* (San Diego: Harvest Books, 1959).

5 *Encyclopedia of Religion,* s.v. "Sacred Space," by Joel Brereton, accessed July 12, 2020, www.encyclopedia.com/environment/encyclopedias-almanacs-transcripts-and-maps /sacred-space.

6 Ellen Badone, "Conventional and Unconventional Pilgrimages: Conceptualizing Sacred Travel in the Twenty-First Century," in *Redefining Pilgrimage: New Perspectives on Historical and Contemporary Pilgrimages,* ed. Anton Pazos (Farnham, UK: Ashgate Publishing, 2014): 26.

7 Belden Lane, *Landscapes of the Sacred: Geography and Narrative in American Spirituality* (Baltimore: Johns Hopkins University Press, 2001).

8 Rudolf Otto, *The Idea of the Holy: An Inquiry Into the Non-Rational Factor in the Idea of the Divine and Its Relation to the Rational,* 3rd ed. (Oxford: Oxford University Press, 1925).

9 Otto, *Idea of the Holy,* 71.

10 Antonio R. Gualtieri, "Landscape, Consciousness, and Culture," *Religious Studies* 19, no. 2 (1983): 167, https://doi.org/10.1017/S0034412500015006.

11 Alan Morinis, ed., *Sacred Journeys: The Anthropology of Pilgrimage,* Contributions to the Study of Anthropology 7 (Santa Barbara: Greenwood Press, 1992), 6.

12 Arnold van Gennep, *The Rites of Passage,* trans. Monika B. Vizedom and Gabrielle L. Caffe (1909; repr., Chicago: University of Chicago Press, 1960).

13 James Mills, "Spiritual Landscapes: A Comparative Study of Burial Mound Sites in the Upper Mississippi River Basin and the Practice of Feng Shui in East Asia" (PhD diss., University of Minnesota, 1992).

14 Joseph M. Cheer, Yaniv Belhassen, and Joanna Kujawa, "The Search for Spirituality in Tourism: Toward a Conceptual Framework for Spiritual Tourism," *Tourism Management Perspectives* 24 (2017): 252–256, https://doi.org/10.1016/j.tmp.2017.07.018.

Chapter 6: Principles for Creating Pilgrimage Pathways

1 Kirsten Bell, "Pilgrims and Progress: The Production of Religious Experience in a Korean Religion," *Nova Religio: The Journal of Alternative and Emergent Religions* 12, no. 1: 83–102.

2 Nan Shepard, *The Living Mountain* (Edinburgh, Scotland: Cannongate Books, 2011), 106.

3 Tony Hiss, "Wonderlust: 'Deep Travel' Opens Our Minds to the Rich Possibilities of Ordinary Experience," *The American Scholar* 79, no. 4 (2010): 52–57.

4 Robert Macfarlane, "Introduction," in *The Living Mountain* by Nan Shepard (Edinburgh, Scotland: Cannongate Books, 2011), xv.

5 Vaclav Cilek, *To Breathe with Birds: A Book of Landscapes,* Penn Studies in Landscape Architecture (Philadelphia: University of Pennsylvania Press, 2015).

6 Victor Turner and Edith Turner, *Image and Pilgrimage in Christian Culture: Anthropological Perspectives* (New York: Columbia University Press, 1978).

7 Francis, Prayer for the Care of Creation (Vatican City: Vatican Press, 2016).

8 Diana Butler Bass, *Grounded: Finding God in the World: A Spiritual Revolution* (San Francisco: Harper One, 2015).

9 Thomas Berry, *The Great Work: Our Way Into the Future* (New York: Harmony/Bell Tower, 1999), 49.

Chapter 7: Implementing New Pilgrimage Pathways

1 Kumi Kato and Ricardo Nicolas Progano, "Spiritual (Walking) Tourism as a Foundation for Sustainable Destination Development: Kumano-ko Pilgrimage, Wakayama, Japan," *Tourism Management Perspectives 24* (2017): 243–251.

BIBLIOGRAPHY

Abbey, Edward. *Desert Solitaire: A Season in the Wilderness.* New York: Touchstone Books, 1990.

Algonquin to Adirondacks Collaborative. "Introducing the A2A Trail—A Pilgrimage for Nature." Algonquin to Adirondacks Collaborative. Accessed 7/24/2019. www.a2acollaborative.org.

Alliance of Religions and Conservation. "Green Pilgrimage Network." Accessed July 12, 2020. www.arcworld.org/projects.asp?projectID=521.

Alliance of Religions and Conservation. "News Archive, January 31, 2012. ARC Discusses Pilgrimage on the BBC's Beyond Belief Programme." Accessed July 12, 2020. www .arcworld.org/news.asp?pageID=517.

Badone, Ellen. "Conventional and Unconventional Pilgrimages: Conceptualizing Sacred Travel in the Twenty-First Century." In *Redefining Pilgrimage: New Perspectives on Historical and Contemporary Pilgrimages,* edited by Anton Pazos, 7–33. Farnham, UK: Ashgate Publishing, 2014.

Bell, Kirsten. "Pilgrims and Progress: The Production of Religious Experience in a Korean Religion." *Nova Religio: The Journal of Alternative and Emergent Religions* 12, no. 1 (2008): 83–102.

Berry, Thomas. *The Great Work: Our Way into the Future.* New York: Harmony/Bell Tower, 1999.

Bhardwaj, Surinder M. "Single Religion Shrines, Multireligion Pilgrimages." *The National Geographical Journal of India* 33, no. 4 (1987): 457–468.

Bremborg, Anna Davidsson. "Creating Sacred Space by Walking in Silence: Pilgrimage in a Late Modern Lutheran Context." *Social Compass* 60, no. 4 (2013): 544–560.

Brown, David. *God and Enchantment of Place: Reclaiming Human Experience.* Oxford: Oxford University Press, 2006.

Bunyan, John. *The Pilgrim's Progress.* Boston: Dent/Dutton, 1954.

Burton-Christie, Douglas. "The Gift of Tears: Loss, Mourning and the Work of Ecological Restoration." *Worldviews* 15 (2011): 29–46.

Butler Bass, Diana. *Grounded: Finding God in the World: A Spiritual Revolution.* San Francisco: Harper One, 2015.

Campo, Juan Eduardo. "American Pilgrimage Landscapes." *Annals of the American Academy of Political and Social Science* 558 (1998): 40–56.

Carreno, Guillermo Salas. "The Glacier, the Rock, the Image: Emotional Experience and Semiotic Diversity at the Quyllurit'i Pilgrimage, Cuzco, Peru." *Signs and Society* 2, no. S1 (2014): S188–S214.

Chaucer, Geoffrey. *The Canterbury Tales.* Edited by Sinan Kökbugur. 1387–1400. Librarius .com.

Cheer, Joseph M., Yaniv Belhassen, and Joanna Kujawa. "The Search for Spirituality in Tourism: Toward a Conceptual Framework for Spiritual Tourism." *Tourism Management Perspectives* 24 (2017): 252–256. https://doi.org/10.1016/j.tmp.2017.07.018.

Cilek, Vaclav. *To Breathe with Birds: A Book of Landscapes.* Penn Studies in Landscape Architecture. Philadelphia: University of Pennsylvania Press, 2015.

Clift, Jean Dalby and Wallace B. Clift. *The Archetype of Pilgrimage: Outer Action with Inner Meaning.* Mahwah, NJ: Paulist Press, 1996.

Coats, Curtis. "Is the Womb Barren? A Located Study of Spiritual Tourism in Sedona, Arizona, and Its Possible Effect on Eco-Consciousness." *Journal for the Study of Religion, Nature and Culture* 2, no. 4 (2008): 483–507.

Cousineau, Phil. *The Art of Pilgrimage: The Seeker's Guide to Making Travel Sacred.* Anniversary ed. San Francisco: Conari Press, 2012.

Danely, Jason. "A Watchful Presence: Aesthetics of Well-Being in a Japanese Pilgrimage." *Ethnos: Journal of Anthropology* 82, no. 1 (2017): 165–192.

Davidson, Linda Kay and David M. Gitlitz. *Pilgrimage: From the Ganges to Graceland.* Santa Barbara: ABC-CLIO, 2002.

Digance, Justine. "Religious and Secular Pilgrimage: Journeys Redolent With Meaning." In *Tourism, Religion and Spiritual Journey,* edited by Dallen J. Timothy and Daniel H. Olsen, 36–49. Abingdon-on-Thames, UK: Routledge, 2006.

DiGiovine, Michael A. *"Apologia pro Turismo:* Breaking Inter- and Intra-Disciplinary Boundaries in the Anthropological Study of Tourism and Pilgrimage." *Journal of Tourism Challenges and Trends* 6, no. 2 (2013): 63–94.

DiGiovine, Michael A. "Pilgrimage: *Communitas* and Contestation, Unity and Difference—An Introduction." *Tourism Review* 59, no. 3 (2011): 247–269.

Duany, Andres, Elizabeth Plater-Zyberk, and Jeff Speck. *Suburban Nation: The Rise of Sprawl and the Decline of the American Dream.* New York: North Point Press, 2000.

Dubisch, Jill. "Healing the Wounds That Are Not Visible": A Vietnam Veterans' Motorcycle Pilgrimage." In *Pilgrimage and Healing,* edited by Jill Dubisch and Michael Winkelman, 135–154. Tucson: University of Arizona Press, 2005.

Dubisch, Jill and Michael Winkelman, eds. *Pilgrimage and Healing.* Tucson: University of Arizona Press, 2005.

Eaton, Leo, dir. *Sacred Journeys with Bruce Feiler.* DVD. Boston: WGBH Educational Foundation: Maya Vision International, 2014.

Eck, Diana. *India: A Sacred Geography.* New York: Harmony Books, 2012.

Eck, Diana. *Banaras: City of Light.* New York: Columbia University Press, 1998.

Eeckhout, Peter. "Change and Permanency on the Coast of Ancient Peru: The Religious Site of Pachacamac." *World Archaeology* 45, no. 1 (2013): 137–160.

Bibliography

Eiseley, Loren. *The Immense Journey*. New York: Vintage Books, 1959.

Eliade, Mircea. *The Sacred and the Profane: The Nature of Religion*. San Diego: Harvest Books, 1959.

Esch, Mary. "Wandering Moose Inspires 400-Mile Cross-Border Trail." Associated Press, August 13, 2016.

Estevez, Emilio, dir. *The Way*. DVD. Barcelona: Filmax; Elixir Films, 2010.

Francis. *Laudato Si' (On Care for Our Common Home)*. Vatican City: Vatican Press, 2015.

Francis. Prayer for the Care of Creation. Vatican City: Vatican Press, 2016.

Gallup. "In Depth: Religion." Accessed July 12, 2020. https://news.gallup.com/poll/1690 /religion.aspx.

Gesler, Wil. "Lourdes: Healing in a Place of Pilgrimage." *Health and Place* 2, no. 2 (1996): 95–105.

Gitlitz, David M. "Old Pilgrimage, New Meanings; New Pilgrimages, Old Forms: From the Ganges to Graceland." In *Redefining Pilgrimage: New Perspectives on Historical and Contemporary Pilgrimages*, edited by Anton Pazos, 33–46. Farnham, UK: Ashgate Publishing, 2014.

Graber, Linda H. *Wilderness as Sacred Space*. Washington, DC: Association of American Geographers, 1976.

Grimshaw, Mike. "Sheilas on the Move? Religion, Spirituality, and Tourism." *Journal of Religious History* 37, no. 4 (2013): 541–552.

Gualtieri, Antonio R. "Landscape, Consciousness, and Culture." *Religious Studies* 19, no. 2 (1983): 161–174. https://doi.org/10.1017/S0034412500015006.

Haigney, Sophie. "How Stone Stacking Wreaks Havoc on National Parks." *New Yorker*, December 2, 2018.

Herrero, Nieves. "Reaching Land's End: New Social Practices in the Pilgrimage to Santiago de Compostela." *International Journal of Iberian Studies* 21, no. 2 (2008): 131–148.

Hiss, Tony. "Wonderlust: 'Deep Travel' Opens Our Minds to the Rich Possibilities of Ordinary Experience." *The American Scholar* 79, no. 4 (2010): 52–57.

Hitchens, Daniel. "Pilgrimage's Progress: One of Britain's Oldest Christian Traditions is Reviving in a Strange New Form." *The Spectator*, July 16, 2016, 22.

Huntsinger, Lynn and Maria Fernandez-Gimenez. "Spiritual Pilgrims at Mount Shasta, California." *The Geographical Review* 90, no. 4 (2000): 536–558.

Ivakhiv, Adrian. "Power Trips: Making Sacred Space through New Age Pilgrimage." In *Handbook of New Age*, edited by Daren Kemp and James R. Lewis, 263–286. Leiden, Netherlands: Brill Publishing, 2007.

Joyce, Rachel. *The Unlikely Pilgrimage of Harold Fry: A Novel*. New York: Random House, 2013.

Kato, Kumi and Ricardo Nicolas Progano. "Spiritual (Walking) Tourism as a Foundation for Sustainable Destination Development: Kumano-ko Pilgrimage, Wakayama, Japan." *Tourism Management Perspectives* 24 (2017): 243–251.

Lane, Belden. *Landscapes of the Sacred: Geography and Narrative in American Spirituality*. Baltimore: Johns Hopkins University Press, 2001.

Least Heat Moon, William. *Blue Highways: A Journey into America.* New York: Little, Brown and Company, 1982.

Lee, Wendy J. N., dir. *Pad Yatra: A Green Odyssey.* DVD. Los Angeles: Good Docs Films, 2013.

Luther, Martin. *To the Christian Nobility of the German Nation.* 1520. Annotated study guide ed. Minneapolis: Fortress Press, 2016.

Macfarlane, Robert. "Rites of Way: Behind the Pilgrimage Revival." *The Guardian,* June 15, 2012, www.theguardian.com.

Mahoney, Rosemary. *The Singular Pilgrim: Travels on Sacred Ground.* New York: Houghton Mifflin Harcourt, 2003.

Mills, James. "Spiritual Landscapes: A Comparative Study of Burial Mound Sites in the Upper Mississippi River Basin and the Practice of Feng Shui in East Asia." PhD diss., University of Minnesota, 1992.

Morinis, Alan, ed. *Sacred Journeys: The Anthropology of Pilgrimage.* Contributions to the Study of Anthropology 7. Santa Barbara: Greenwood Press, 1992.

Nasr, Seyyed Hossein. "Pilgrimage: The Heart of Islam." Lecture at the Washington National Cathedral, Washington, DC, December 2, 2003.

Notermans, Catrien. "Loss and Healing: A Marian Pilgrimage in Secular Dutch Society." *Ethnology* 46, no. 3 (2007): 1–17.

Olstad, Tyra. *Zen of the Plains: Experiencing Wild Western Places.* Southwestern Nature Writing Series. Denton: University of North Texas Press, 2014.

Otto, Rudolf. *The Idea of the Holy: An Inquiry into the Non-Rational Factor in the Idea of the Divine and Its Relation to the Rational.* 3rd ed. Oxford: Oxford University Press, 1925.

Pazos, Anton M., ed. *Redefining Pilgrimage: New Perspectives on Historical and Contemporary Pilgrimages.* Farnham, UK: Ashgate Publishing, 2014.

Pew Research Center. "America's Changing Religious Landscape." Accessed July 12, 2020. www.pewforum.org/2015/05/12/americas-changing-religious-landscape.

Pew Research Center. "In U.S., Decline of Christianity Continues at a Rapid Pace." Accessed July 12, 2020. www.pewforum.org/2019/10/17/in-u-s-decline-of-christianity-continues-at-rapid-pace.

Prorok, Carolyn V. "Transplanting Pilgrimage Traditions in the Americas." *Geographical Review* 93, no. 3 (2003): 283–307.

Putnam, Robert. "Bowling Alone: America's Declining Social Capital." *Journal of Democracy* 6, no. 1 (1995): 65–78.

Rasmussen, Larry L. *Earth-Honoring Faith: Religious Ethics in a New Key.* Oxford: Oxford University Press, 2013.

Reader, Ian. *Making Pilgrimages: Meaning and Practice in Shikoku.* Honolulu: University of Hawai'i Press, 2006.

Rosenzweig, Michael L. *Win-Win Ecology: How the Earth's Species Can Survive in the Midst of Human Enterprise.* Oxford: Oxford University Press, 2003.

Run for the Wall. "Run for the Wall: We Ride For Those Who Can't." Accessed July 12, 2020. https://rftw.us.

Sallnow, Michael J. *Pilgrims of the Andes: Regional Cults in Cusco.* Washington, DC: Smithsonian Institution Press, 1987.

Scham, Sandra. "The World's First Temple." *Archaeology,* November/December 2008: 22–27.

Schmidt, William S. "Transformative Pilgrimage." *Journal of Spirituality in Mental Health* 11 (2009): 66–77.

Shepard, Nan. *The Living Mountain.* Edinburgh, Scotland: Cannongate Books, 2011.

Siddiqi, Bulbul. "'Purification of Self': *Ijtema* as a New Islamic Pilgrimage." *European Journal of Economic and Political Studies* 3 (2010): 133–150.

Silverman, Helaine. "The Archaeological Identification of an Ancient Peruvian Pilgrimage Center." *World Archaeology* 26, no. 1 (1994): 1–18.

Smith, Jonathon Z. *To Take Place: Toward Theory in Ritual.* Chicago: University of Chicago Press, 1987.

Smith, Roff. "Before Stonehenge." *National Geographic,* August 2014: 26–51.

Smyers, Karen A. "Inari Pilgrimage: Following One's Own Path on the Mountain." *Japanese Journal of Religious Studies* 24, no. 3/4 (1997): 427–452.

Solnit, Rebecca. *Wanderlust: A History of Walking.* New York: Viking-Penguin, 2000.

Steinbeck, John. *Travels with Charley: In Search of America.* New York: Viking, 1962.

Stoddard, Robert H. and Alan Morinis, eds. *Sacred Places, Sacred Spaces: The Geography of Pilgrimages.* Geoscience and Man 34. Baton Rouge: Louisiana State University, 1997.

Timothy, Dallen J. and Daniel H. Olsen eds. *Tourism, Religion and Spiritual Journeys.* Abingdon-on-Thames, UK: Routledge Publishing, 2006.

Turner, Victor W. *The Ritual Process: Structure and Anti-Structure.* London: Aldine Publishing, 1969.

Turner, Victor W. and Edith Turner. *Image and Pilgrimage in Christian Culture: Anthropological Perspectives.* New York: Columbia University Press, 1978.

Van Gennep, Arnold. *The Rites of Passage.* Translated by Monika B. Vizedom and Gabrielle L. Caffe. Chicago: University of Chicago Press, 1960. First published in French in 1909.

Welch, Sally. "Pilgrimage." YouTube video, 57:12. Accessed July 12, 2020. www.youtube.com/watch?v=8OiFcneW3tw.

Williams, Allison. "Spiritual Therapeutic Landscapes and Healing: A Case Study of St. Anne de Beaupre, Quebec, Canada." *Social Science and Medicine* 70 (2010): 1633–1640.

Zelinsky, Wilbur. "The Uniqueness of the American Religious Landscape." *Geographical Review* 91, no. 3 (2001): 565–585.

INDEX

C

ABOUT THE AUTHOR

JAMES MILLS is a professor at SUNY Oneonta, where he served as the director of the Environmental Sciences Program for eight years and helped create a new major in environmental sustainability. He currently teaches regional courses on Asia, the Geography of Culture and Environment, and a course entitled Religion, Spirit, and Environment. Mills received an undergraduate degree in natural resource management from the University of Wisconsin, Madison, and a doctorate in geography from the University of Minnesota, Twin Cities. Over the course of his personal and academic career, he has visited pilgrimage destinations across East and Southeast Asia, the Middle East, Europe, and the United States.

About North Atlantic Books

North Atlantic Books (NAB) is an independent, nonprofit publisher committed to a bold exploration of the relationships between mind, body, spirit, and nature. Founded in 1974, NAB aims to nurture a holistic view of the arts, sciences, humanities, and healing. To make a donation or to learn more about our books, authors, events, and newsletter, please visit www.northatlanticbooks.com.

North Atlantic Books is the publishing arm of the Society for the Study of Native Arts and Sciences, a 501(c)(3) nonprofit educational organization that promotes cross-cultural perspectives linking scientific, social, and artistic fields. To learn how you can support us, please visit our website.